CASSANDRA DIAS

Richly Stitched LANDSCAPE EMBROIDERY

Mastering Thread Painted Scenes

stashBOOKS®
an imprint of C&T Publishing

Publisher: Amy Barrett-Daffin

Creative Director: Gailen Runge

Senior Editor: Roxane Cerda

Editor: Madison Moore

Technical Editor: Sarah Ruiz

Cover/Book Designer: April Mostek

Production Coordinator: Zinnia Heinzmann

Illustrator: Kirstie Pettersen

Photography Coordinator: Rachel Ackley

Front cover photography by Cassandra Dias

Photography by Cassandra Dias, unless otherwise noted

Published by Stash Books, an imprint of C&T Publishing, Inc., P.O. Box 1456, Lafayette, CA 94549

Library of Congress Cataloging-in-Publication Data

Names: Dias, Cassandra, 1985- author

Title: Richly stitched landscape embroidery : mastering thread painted scenes / Cassandra Dias.

Description: Lafayette, CA : Stash Books, an imprint of C&T Publishing, [2026] | Summary: "Learn how to stitch majestic, swirling landscapes bursting with rich, thread-painted texture! Richly Stitched Landscape Embroidery teaches readers how to stitch stunning textile masterpieces with ten tutorials and seven patterns"-- Provided by publisher

Identifiers: LCCN 2025040140 | ISBN 9781644035856 trade paperback | ISBN 9781644035863 ebook

Subjects: LCSH: Embroidery--Patterns | Cross-stitch--Patterns | BISAC: CRAFTS & HOBBIES / Needlework / Embroidery | CRAFTS & HOBBIES / Nature Crafts

Classification: LCC TT771 .D537 2026 | DDC 746.44/3041--dc23/eng/20250929

LC record available at https://lccn.loc.gov/2025040140

Printed in China

10 9 8 7 6 5 4 3 2 1

DEDICATION

For my Dad, who wasn't able to actually see my dream of being an artist become a reality, but who I know has been right here with me every step of the way.

ACKNOWLEDGMENTS

First, Aunt Kathy: I'm not sure I would have ever tried my hand at embroidery if you hadn't sent me that old bag of DMC embroidery floss years ago. Who would have known it would evolve into this? Thank you so much!

To my family and friends who have supported me from the very beginning of my embroidery journey, and who have been excited for me throughout the process of writing this book: your advice and encouraging words have truly been appreciated. I am so grateful to have such an amazing support system.

Anthony, thank you for believing in me. For being my sounding board and offering your creative perspective, for your understanding, for your hugs when it got hard. For being someone I can always count on. I love you!

Aiden and Amara, the looks of awe on your faces when I told you, "Mama is going to write a book," is something that I carried with me through this entire process, and you two being proud of me means everything. Remember, you can do hard things!

Mom, your unwavering faith in me is such a comfort—constantly reassuring me of how strong I am and what I am capable of. Thanks for always being there for me.

To Madison, my editor, your guidance throughout what has been a huge learning experience for me has made such a massive impact! I literally would have been so lost in all this without you. On that same note, to the amazing women on the C&T production team who worked so closely with me: thank you all so much for helping me to bring my vision to life!

To the talented artists that originally motivated me, those that continue to inspire me to pursue my own art, and the wonderful social media community I've become a part of that embraces my creativity in such a positive way: I am filled with gratitude for the way you embolden me.

And, a special thanks to DMC for the generous contribution of the many, *many* thread colors used in the creation of these projects, to Nurge for gifting me beautiful display hoops, and to Kate from Modern Hoopla for supplying me with the exceptionally crafted handmade embroidery frames. I genuinely appreciate your kindness and willingness to help.

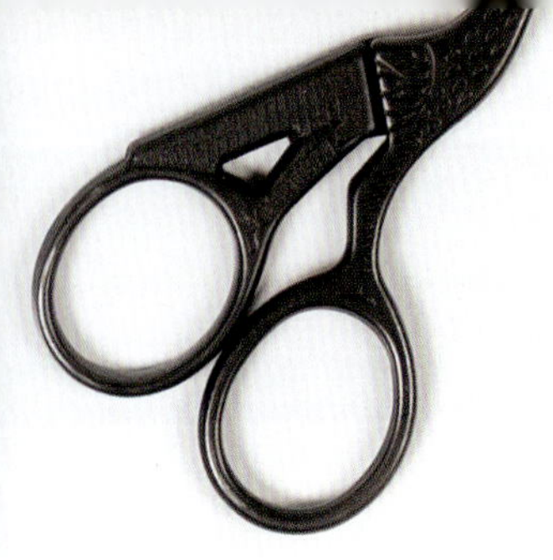

Contents

LANDSCAPE ELEMENT TUTORIALS

LANDSCAPE PROJECTS

Introduction

Hello! I am so excited to share my passion for hand embroidery with you! I absolutely fell in love with thread painting during the early days of my embroidery journey, and in this book, you will learn how to apply this method to landscape scenes.

Photo by Anthony Dias

Thread painting, also known as needle painting or silk shading, is an embroidery technique that melds basic hand embroidery stitches with blending and shading colors, resulting in the appearance of a traditional painting or realistic imagery. Within these chapters, I break the process down into manageable steps and work on a small, approachable scale. You will get to practice and sharpen your thread painting skills through a variety of nature-inspired tutorials and full-size landscape projects, each explained and pictured step-by-step.

My goal is to turn you on to an art form you may never have believed you could do, and that embroidery becomes something you don't want to put down! Whether you go on to continue creating landscapes, or take these fundamentals of thread painting and implement them in whatever subject matter you prefer, I hope this technique brings you joy, helps you settle your mind and body, eases your stress, and allows you regain possession of your you-time—as it has for me.

So, go get yourself a nice cup (or glass) of something, grab your supplies, and let's get started!

Photo by Anthony Dias

Tools & Materials

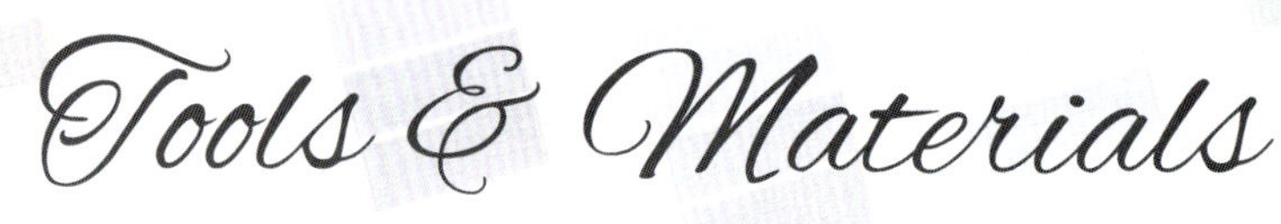

Gather the proper materials for your project before you get started. The items you need for thread painting embroidery are pretty basic and can easily be found at your local craft store or online (if you don't have them on hand already!).

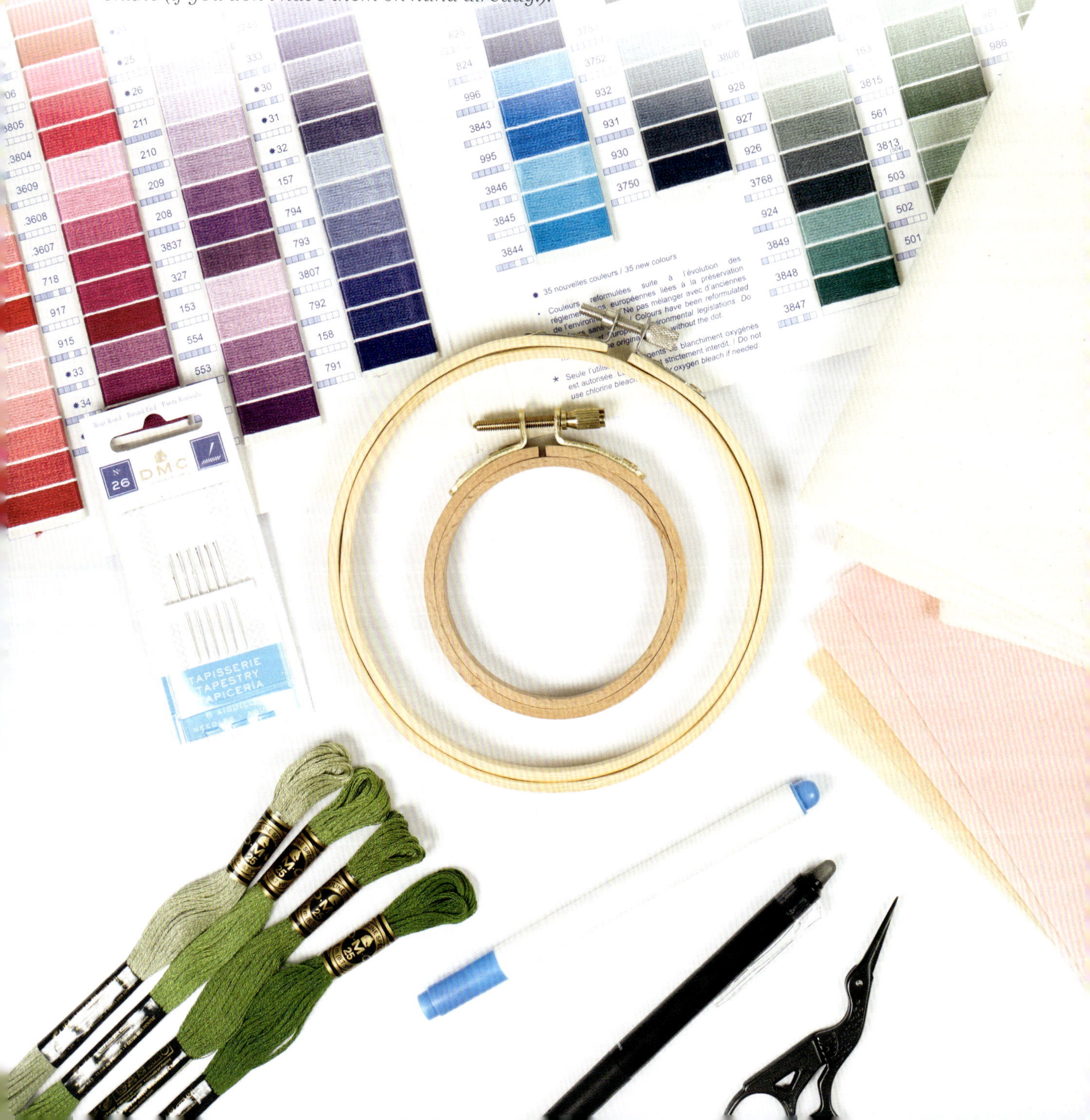

GENERAL HAND EMBROIDERY MATERIALS

Fabric

When it comes to choosing the right fabric as a base for your hand embroidery project, there are different factors you have to consider. How heavily stitched is the design? What types of stitches will I be using? How do I plan on displaying the finished piece? For the projects in this book, a tightly-woven, medium-weight plain weave fabric works best.

100% cotton medium-weight duck canvas is my personal favorite and makes an ideal stitching surface because it's sturdy and the fabric threads typically fill the weave completely while providing stability for the high number of stitches.

Needles

I've found I don't like using traditional embroidery needles. Instead, I opt for tapestry or chenille needles because I prefer the larger eye that can easily accommodate multiple threads. Most of the time, I use and recommend a size 26 tapestry needle, which typically has a rounded end. If you need something to push through thick layers of stitches, I suggest a sharp-ended chenille needle.

Thread

I recommend stranded cotton embroidery floss so you can use a variable number of threads for different parts of each project. I exclusively use DMC 6-stranded embroidery floss because there is a massive range of colors, and the thread is high-quality.

Hoops

A basic bamboo hoop is a lightweight yet durable option that is easy to use. The projects in this book usually recommend a 5″ (12.7cm) bamboo hoop for stitching. After stitching, I prefer to display the finished pieces in a 3″ (7.6cm) display hoop (see Display Materials, right).

Scissors

You need a pair of embroidery scissors with a small, sharp point that allows you to get in close to the base fabric and easily snip small threads. A pair of fabric scissors also helps with preparing the base or backing fabric.

TRANSFER TOOLS

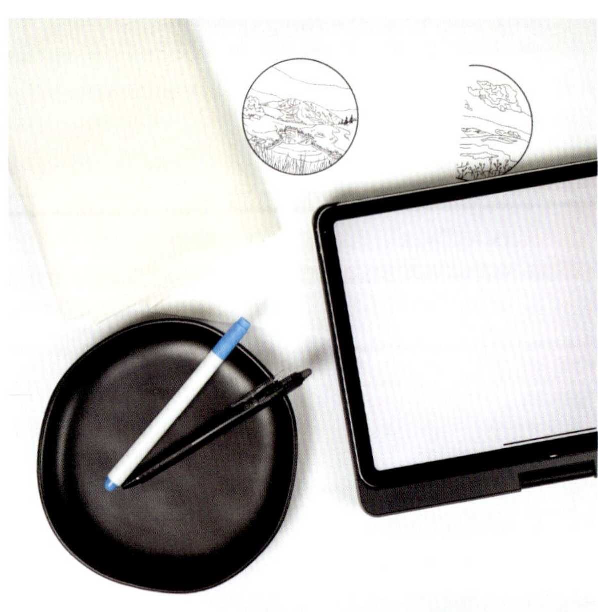

Determining which transfer tools are the right ones for your project depends mostly on your own personal preference. You will figure out which tools you like to work with through practice. I prefer to trace my designs. Transfer markers and pens, whether they are water-soluble or thermo-sensitive, are the easiest transfer method for my process.

Water-Soluble Markers

Water-soluble markers, such as the blue marking pen by EZ Quilting, erase easily by getting the marks wet. They're a great choice for designs with less detail, as the marker tips are thicker and can be difficult to use with intricate linework.

Thermo-Sensitive Pens

Thermo-sensitive pens, like the FriXon Erasable Gel Ink Pen by Pilot, have finer points so they are capable of better capturing more detailed designs, and the ink can be erased with the heat from a hair dryer or an iron. I use Pilot's FriXion Synergy Clicker erasable pen with an extra fine (.5mm) point.

Light Source

A light source is an essential tool for tracing a design onto fabric. Print the pattern onto paper at the correct size, then layer it with the base fabric over a bright light source. A window works well if it's sunny outside; tape the printed design to the glass, then tape the fabric on top. You can also use an iPad as a lightbox, or you can purchase a standard tabletop lightbox to use anytime.

DISPLAY MATERIALS

Once I've finished stitching, I always look forward to perfecting a piece by making those small decisions about how to tie everything together.

Display Hoop

Embroidery hoops come in all sorts of shapes, sizes, and materials, and are the most common way to display needlework. The key is to find a hoop that rounds out the completed piece. Whether you choose one that adds balance, refinement, or personality, it should never take away too much attention from the work itself. I really like Sherbo's solid beech hoops with brass accents, or Nurge's Flexi Hoops that give a sense of sophistication with their classic wood grain look and a decorative hanging hook.

Felt

Felt is my fabric of choice for covering the backs of my hoops to hide and protect the back of the stitching. Choosing a color that corresponds with the piece can make it a nice finishing touch.

Shadow Box

I love displaying embroideries in a shadow box from Lawrence Frames because the pieces are shielded behind glass, which protects against dust and other environmental elements. Additionally, the deep frame of a shadow box allows for both hanging or propping up the artwork.

Embroidery Frame

Frames, like display hoops, should be chosen to complement the finished embroidery. The color, shape, and size of your frame can easily enhance the overall visual appeal of an embroidery work. I recently discovered handmade wooden embroidery frames by Modern Hoopla and really appreciate the thoughtful designs that allow you to conveniently insert your work into the frame without taking it out of its hoop.

HELPFUL OPTIONAL ITEMS

Hoop Stand

Anytime the opportunity to relieve some of the stress from your back or hands while embroidering presents itself, take it! I tend to use my Nurge tabletop hoop stand when working on pieces that are heavily adorned with French knots, which are easiest to create with both hands available.

Thimble

When developing a piece with lots of layers, I sometimes need a thimble to protect my fingertips and make it easier to push my needle through the work. Thimble pads (from Colonial Needle Co.) are super adhesive, reusable, and less bulky than a metal thimble.

DMC Thread Color Card

A threaded color card comes in handy when trying to decide which colors to use in a project. Being able to see all the colors DMC has to offer without having to drag yourself to the craft store is a real time saver!

Color & Design

During the conception stage of an embroidery project, you get to decide all the details that will eventually come together to create your vision! You will choose your subject matter, consider which stitches work best for bringing the elements to life, determine the size, draw the design, select the colors you want to incorporate, and figure out how you would like to display the finished piece.

WORKING FROM A REFERENCE PHOTO

I typically use reference photos for my pieces because they capture more detail than my memory can recall or that my own imagination can come up with. I have found the best references are photos of places I have been to or would like to visit, because I get to relive or imagine my time there while I'm stitching. When using a reference photo to create a design, freehand drawing directly onto the fabric while studying the image will encourage you to take more creative liberties with the design. On the other hand, tracing directly from the image is a great way to capture all the details.

Gather Inspiration

I find that taking photos of nature while I'm out on walks or hikes or traveling is so helpful to come back to later on when I want to develop a new pattern.

CREATING YOUR OWN DESIGN

Your landscape design should include some basic compositional fundamentals. Having a background, middle, and foreground helps create depth in a piece. You also want to note which direction the light source is coming from and keep the slant of your shadows consistent throughout. Being strategic about where you place focal points can help support the natural flow of the composition and create movement throughout your work.

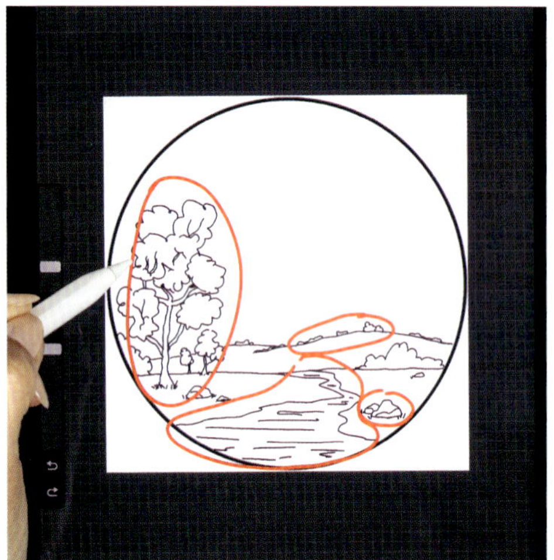

Deciding Which Elements To Incorporate

Once you have decided the type of landscape you want to create, think about the different natural elements you might want to place into the scene and which stitches will be used for them. Working with stitches you enjoy is a large part of what makes thread painting so satisfying, so be mindful of which ones you want to include ahead of time.

Sketching It Out

A visual aid like a sketch is helpful for developing a design, as it's something that can be modified and reworked as you see fit. Coming up with some rough sketches of your scene will allow you to see what it will look like in the hoop. At this time, decide if you'd like the stitching to go all the way to the edge of the display hoop, so that no base fabric shows (this is how I mount my own works), and plan your design accordingly. I like to develop my designs using Procreate.

Small Scale Pieces

There are so many stitches involved in creating a thread painting embroidery, so I enjoy working on a smaller scale. I get the gratification of completing projects faster than I would had I been working on a larger piece.

SELECTING COLORS

To make a color plan, I try to match my thread colors just by comparing a photo to my color card.

Choose or match floss colors for your design in natural light in order to see the colors accurately. Dim and certain artificial lighting can throw off the true color of the threads, and nothing is worse than making progress on a piece only to realize after the fact that the colors are wrong.

Pay attention to the shadows and highlights in your design, as shadows aren't just blacks and greys, and highlights can be influenced by surrounding colors and other environmental factors. Often, the darkest shadows in my pieces are midnight blues and deep browns. In contrast, the highlights in many of my works are yellows and pinks. The range of colors and vibrancy depends on the light source and time of day depicted in the scene.

Finding the right colors for the subtle halftones—the parts of the lit scenery in neither the highlighted or shadowed sections—can be simplified by using the DMC Color Card. In nature, greens, blues, and browns are the most predominant, so having a variety of shades in each of those colors makes choosing your palette easier.

When it comes to using the colors you've chosen (or to those I have recommended for the projects in this book), don't feel bound to your initial selection. I always end up adding more colors or omitting others while I'm stitching. It's all about using the shades that feel right to you!

Embroidery Techniques & Tips

The techniques and tips discussed in this chapter are all things that I have learned along the way throughout my own embroidery journey.

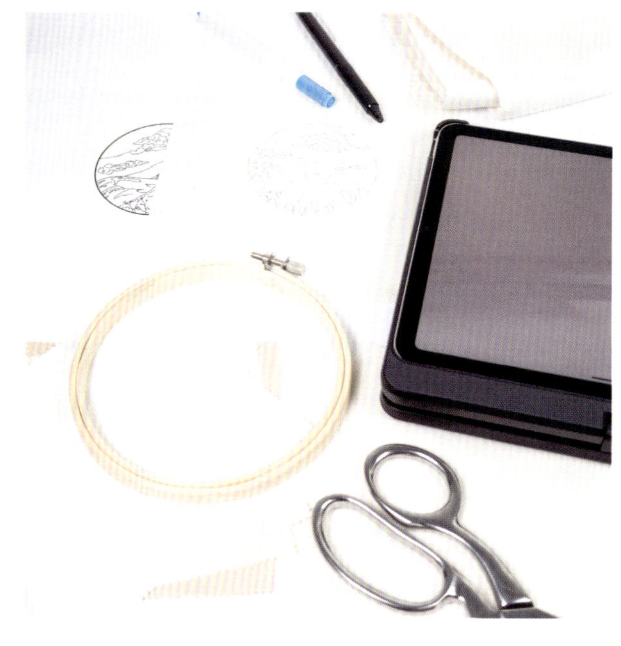

TRANSFERRING DESIGNS

Whether freehand drawing or tracing, getting your design onto your fabric is the final step before you get to start stitching. I have transferred all the patterns in this book onto my fabric by tracing them with an extra fine point thermo-sensitive pen (see Transfer Tools page 10).

USING THREAD

Pull the floss from the side of the skein with the number tag on it (not the logo tag). To separate the strands, loosely pinch the threads in one hand, and pull the number of strands you need straight up and out of the group.

If you need a larger number of strands but it's hard to pull them through the work, use half the number of strands you need, and double them on the needle, pulling the tails to meet. So, if you need 4 strands, separate 2 strands and stitch with them doubled.

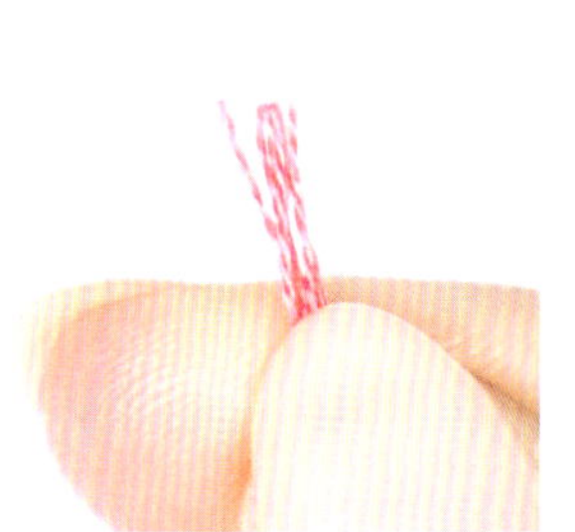

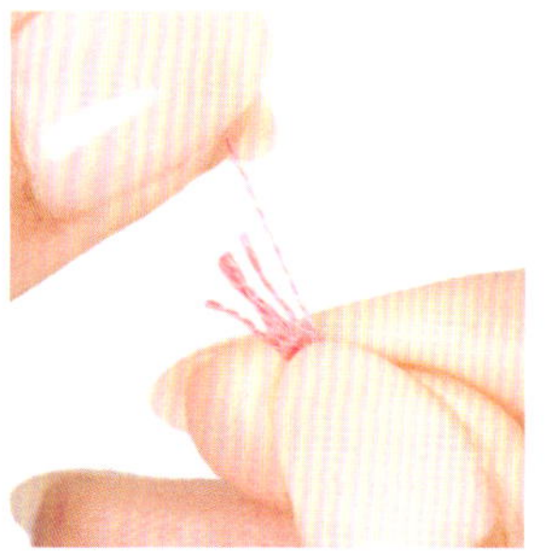

Running Out of Thread

When you run out of thread on the front side of the work, rethread the needle using a separate single strand folded in half (two loose ends coming out the same side) to create a catcher loop. A

Stitch down into the fabric where you would have continued the stitch that ran out of thread. As you pull down through the fabric, catch the end of the thread tail with the loop. Then, pull the loop all the way through, taking the tail with it. Rethread the needle normally and continue stitching. B C

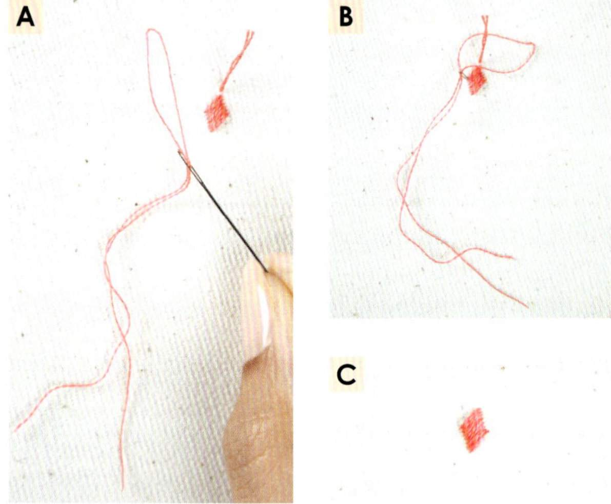

Tying Off Ends

When thread painting, it is not necessary to knot threads on the back of your piece. I have found that the loose threads stay put because all the overlapping stitching creates a secure matrix on the back of the piece. Instead, I simply snip the strands, leaving about ¾″ (2cm) tails. After a while, other stitches will overlap and secure them against the back. If you prefer, you can thread the tails through the existing stitching, and then snip off the excess.

ORT Jar

ORT stands for “old random threads.” Having a jar or container to store thread scraps is so helpful if you need a small piece of a color you’ve already used. Displaying it in your workspace also serves as a visual reminder of all the hard work you’ve put into creating your pieces!

PREPARING THE HOOP

It's essential to pull the base fabric evenly taut in the hoop in order to prevent any puckering or warping in the design once you start stitching.

Consider making sure the warp (the vertical lengthwise support threads of a fabric) and the weft (the horizontal crosswise thread that is woven over and under the warp threads) of the base fabric are straight in the hoop. It's an aesthetic choice, but it can also serve to help keep the horizon line and other elements of the piece straight.

I find it helpful to take a photo of the design drawn on the fabric just in case I stitch over areas or small details, and I can't remember what is supposed to go where. It can also be helpful to photograph the design just in case the pattern gets misplaced or damaged.

THREAD PAINTING

The thought of thread painting may initially seem like a big or slow undertaking, but you will find that it becomes something you really don't want to put down! It's gratifying to the point of being addictive, due to the fact that you aren't confined by a strict stitching plan. You have the freedom to follow your intuition and place your stitches where you want. The satisfying blending of colors and the repetitive motions of your stitches also provide a meditative quality that really makes creating a thread painting an enjoyable process.

I generally like to work from top to bottom and from background to foreground of a piece. This makes achieving the overlap of foreground over background easier. If you can have multiple colors threaded on multiple needles at once, it can save you time and make it easier to remember which colors go where. All examples in this section use 2 strands of floss.

Blending & Mixing Colors

The way you choose to blend threads and colors will produce different effects, from concealing individual stitches to giving flat elements a 3D appearance. Sometimes, in order to get a more seamless gradient, it can be helpful to thread the 2 colors you are blending through the needle at the same time.

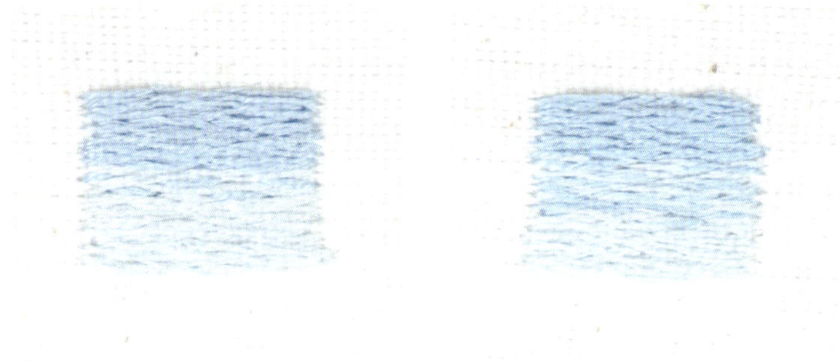

2 colors blended with long and short stitch and straight stitches

Stitching with 2 colors on the needle at the same time in the center of the gradient. Use 1 strand of each color for 2 strands total.

Short Stitches vs. Long Stitches

It's interesting how stitches of different lengths can change the look and texture of your work. I try to use the same length for the stitches throughout the majority of a piece, but there are certain elements that require the use of longer or shorter stitches.

Short stitches work well for foliage and smaller details that are closer to the foreground.

Long stitches work well for skies, grass, calm water, and elements that are farther in the background.

Creating Movement

To stitch a smooth curved shape, gradually slant the stitches to follow the path of the curve, and slowly shorten the stitch length the more the path curves. Blend highlights and shadows into a curve to create additional movement.

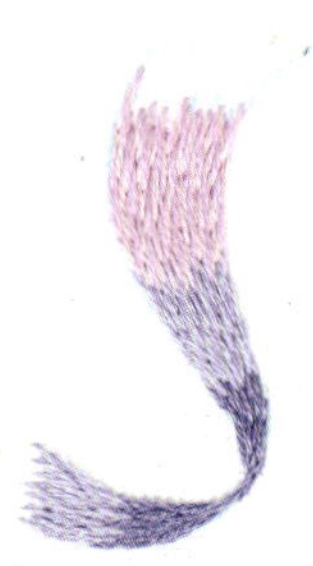

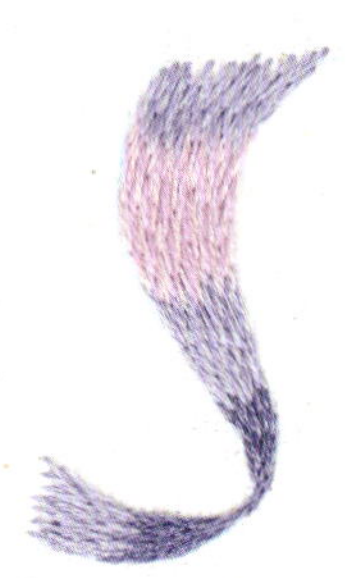

Creating Depth

Integrating elements such as trees and bushes can help add depth to a landscape design. Colors and textures also play a subtle yet effective role in adding depth to a piece. Colors that are closer to the foreground tend to be more saturated than colors that are farther away.

Diminishing the scale of a specific element can also create the illusion of depth. For example, having larger trees rooted in the foreground and stitching a line of smaller ones in the background will easily shift the perspective.

Color saturation and scale diminish moving from foreground to background.

Textured foreground stitching over smoother background stitching.

Flatter and smoother surfaces far off in the background, and rougher, more detailed textures close to the front of the piece can also create the desired effect.

I am a big fan of overlapping layers and adding generous areas of decorative stitches like French knots to the foreground. The elements that are further in the background should be stitched first, behind these front layers.

FINISHING THE HOOP

You've completed stitching your piece! Now you need to finish it in a way that both preserves and presents the piece in the best possible way.

Display

When I've completed a piece, I always like to transfer my work to a smaller display hoop so that no base fabric is visible (though be aware: a small perimeter of the stitching will be hidden too). See Display Materials (page 11) for more on choosing a display method.

Plan Ahead

If you are planning to cover the back of the hoop with felt, complete the first part of Step 1 of Adding Felt (right) before transferring your work to the smaller display hoop.

Closing the Back: Running Stitch

1. Center and secure your work in the display hoop, making sure to pull the fabric taut around the edges as you tighten the screw. Trim the fabric to at least 1″ (2.5cm) around the whole perimeter. **A**

2. Using 2 strands of thread, stitch a running stitch ⅜″ (1cm) in length (straight stitches with gaps between them) in and out of the fabric about ⅜″ (1cm) from the edge. Continue around the entire hoop. Make sure both thread tails are on the front side. **B**

3. Flip the hoop over and pull both thread tails, cinching the fabric. Tie the 2 tails in a knot, keeping the thread taut. Snip the excess. **C**

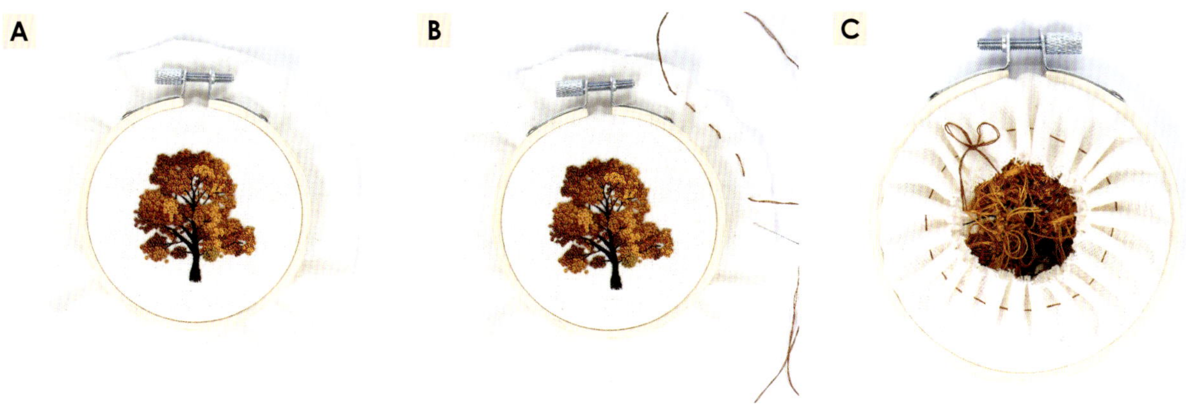

Adding Felt

Placing a barrier over the back of your work protects all those tied-off threads and the piece from dust and other environmental elements.

1. Trace the inside of the inner hoop onto felt with a water soluble blue marker. Cut out the circle, and center it on the back of the piece. **D**

2. Use 2 strands and about 2 arm lengths of thread to thread the needle. Bring the needle up through the base fabric leaving a 1½″ (3.8cm) tail. Tuck the tail behind the felt. Use straight stitches to attach the felt to the cinched backing fabric. **E**

3. Continue stitching all the way around the felt circle. Secure the end of the thread with small satin stitches onto the base fabric below the felt. **F**

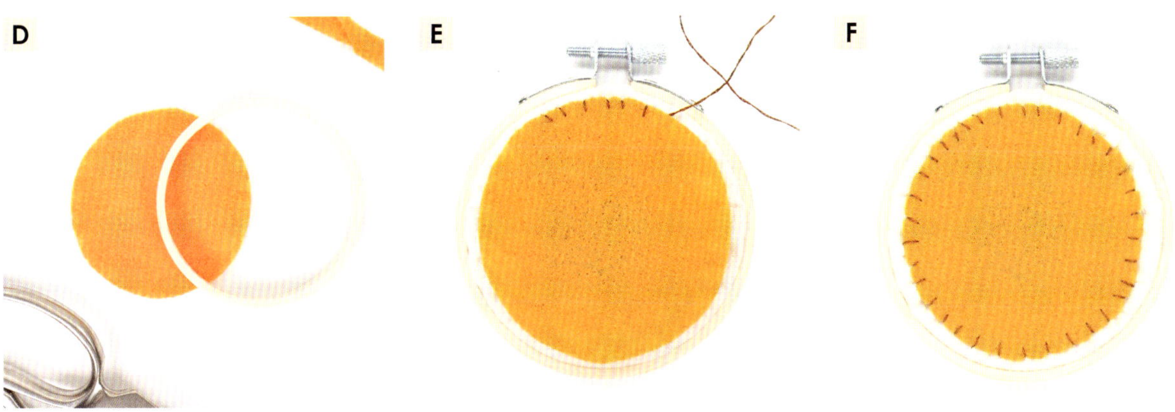

WORKSPACE & PROCESS

Having an area devoted to your embroidery is a great way to stay productive. When I first started, I was stitching on the couch with a coffee table pulled up next to me. And, although it was comfortable (which you definitely want to be), it wasn't the best place to stay focused.

Having all your tools and materials on hand in one place makes the process of creating easier, as you won't have to stop what you're doing midway to go find what you need. Once you are immersed in a project, having to pull your attention away from your work is such a detriment to your creative flow.

When I have tried working in dim or artificial lighting, I would come back to my piece the next day and realize the colors I used weren't what I thought they were. Unpicking threads and re-doing sections was so tedious! Now, I always work in a well-lit room with natural light.

Set Aside Time

Embroidery has been very beneficial to my mental health. It gives me a chance to quiet all the thoughts running through my mind and to focus on the task at hand. I try to sit and work on my pieces around the same time every day, which allows me to make steady progress on whatever project I'm working on. If a daily break to embroider isn't in the cards for you, be intentional about giving yourself opportunities to stitch whenever time does allow.

Don't Be Afraid of A Challenge

Choosing a design or reference photo you are a little intimidated by is a great way to learn about yourself as an embroidery artist. You will find that you are forced to problem solve as you work your way through the piece. Push yourself out of your comfort zone every now and then, and be rewarded with a confidence boost when you succeed!

Sometimes, the imperfections in a piece can become the most endearing parts, especially if you are new to embroidery. Making mistakes is the best way to discover your creative voice. You'll learn if you prefer your stitches neat or more free-flowing, what color combinations you gravitate towards, and what stitches you like and dislike creating.

If I am really bothered by a mistake, I find that it's easier to blend the mistake away with additional stitches instead of unpicking it and starting over.

Create What You Love

If you don't like the subject matter you are embroidering, then your heart won't fully be in it. And, really, what's the point of that? Figuring out what you really love to embroider makes the stitching process so much more satisfying.

The most important thing is to make sure you are enjoying the process! Embroidery should be a relaxing activity. This medium can be easily set down then picked back up again later. If you are not enjoying your time spent stitching, or are having trouble creating, take a breath, take a break, and come back to it when you can.

Stitch Library

The basic stitches in this chapter will be used together to produce embroidered scenes that possess the likeness of traditional paintings! Practice with 2 strands of floss.

STRAIGHT STITCH

This is the most basic of the hand embroidery stitches, and one that is the foundation of many other types of stitches.

1. Bring the needle up through the fabric at the starting point of the first stitch, then put it back down through the fabric at least 1cm away (or desired stitch length). A

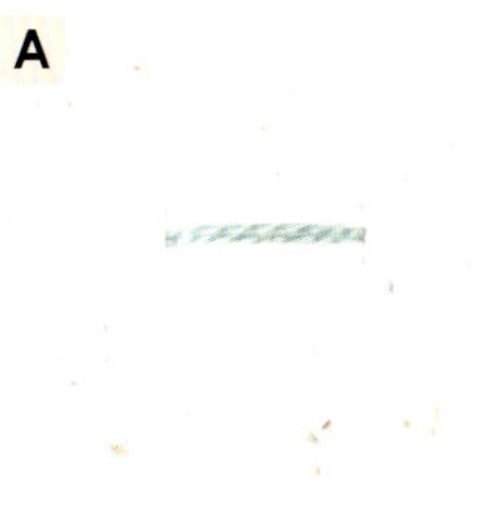

BACK STITCH

The back stitch is another classic hand embroidery stitch that is commonly used to add bordering or filling details.

1. Create a straight stitch.

2. Bring the needle up through the fabric the same stitch length away, then insert the needle back down into the same hole as the end of the first stitch. Repeat to make a line of stitches. B C

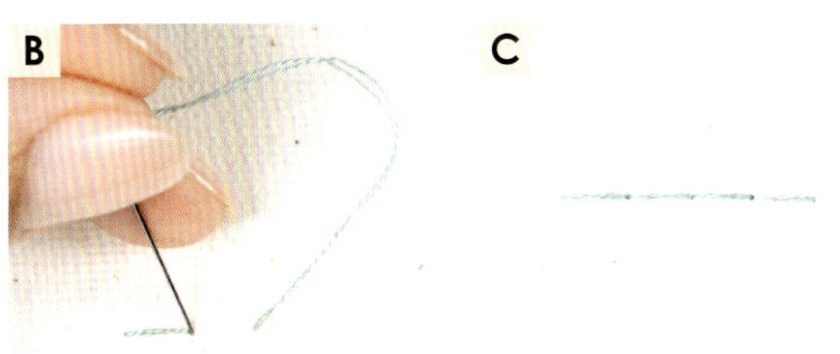

SPLIT STITCH

The split stitch is generally used for outlining and creating stems and branches. I also like to use split stitch interchangeably with split back stitch for filling areas with color.

1. Create a straight stitch.

2. To begin the next stitch, bring the needle up through the middle of the previous stitch, splitting the strands, then stitch back down through the fabric to create a straight stitch of the same length. Repeat to make a line of stitches. D E

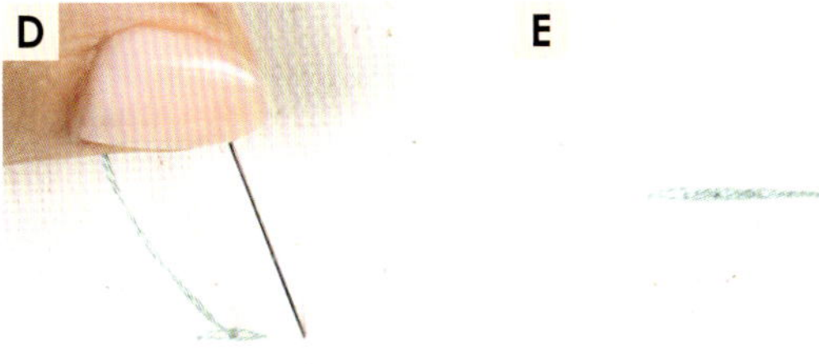

SPLIT BACK STITCH

Split back stitch is a combination of the back stitch and the split stitch. I often use this stitch interchangeably with split stitch when creating branches, edging borders of hills or mountains, or in tandem with long and short stitches for filling areas with color.

1. Create a straight stitch.

2. To begin the next stitch, bring the needle up through the fabric at a distance of half the desired stitch length. Then, insert the needle down through the center of the previous stitch, splitting the strands, or going through a single strand if only using 1 strand of floss. Repeat to make a line of stitches. A B

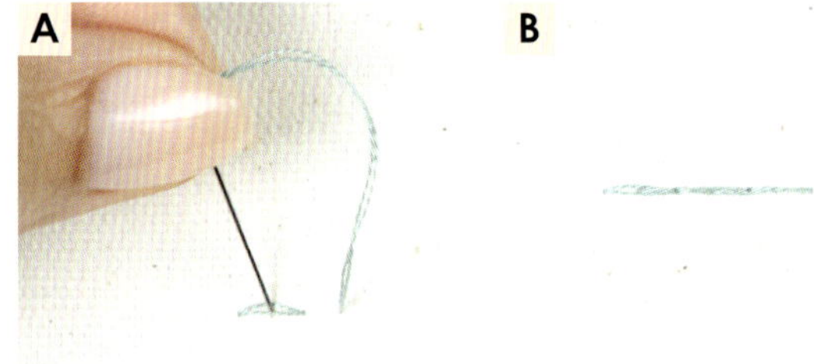

LONG AND SHORT STITCH

Long and short stitch is a blending technique that uses straight stitches of different lengths to create gradients of different colors or fill patches with solid color. It's the primary stitch used in thread painting.

1. Create straight stitches of varying lengths, working across the area to be filled. C

2. Add in the next color with more straight stitches of various lengths, blending with the previous stitches. D

3. Repeat with any remaining colors, making the final stitches end at the end of the section. E

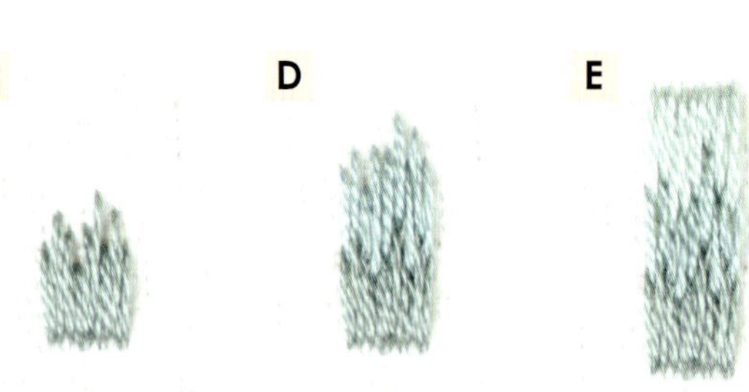

SATIN STITCH

Satin stitch is generally used for filling in areas with solid color. I mainly use it to fill small, flat surfaces, such as sections of rock face or mountain gullies.

1. Bring the needle up at one side of the space to be filled. Bring the needle down directly opposite on the other side of the space, creating a straight stitch across the whole area. F

2. Bring the needle back up next to where you started the previous stitch, and create a parallel straight stitch right next to it. Repeat until the space is filled. G

FRENCH KNOT

French knots are most often used for creating foliage and flowers in landscape thread paintings and add texture and dimension to a piece.

1. Bring the needle up in the spot where the French knot should be, and wrap the thread around the needle with your non-dominant hand. Wrap once for smaller knots, and up to 4 times for larger knots. **A**

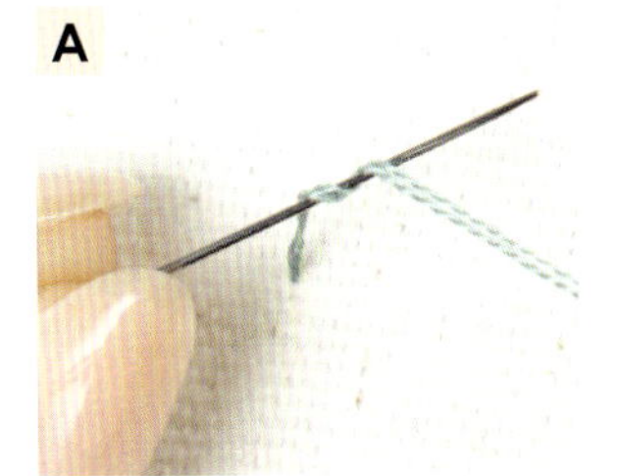
A

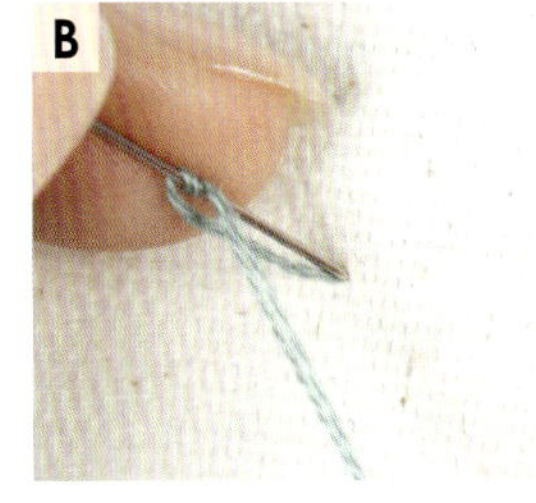
B

Knot Size

For a single-loop French knot, wrap the needle once. For a double-loop French knot, wrap the needle twice.

2. While keeping the thread taut and close to your work, guide the needle back down into the fabric right next to where the needle came up. **B**

3. Pull the needle through, and the knot will start to form. Continue to hold the tension of the thread with your non-dominant hand. Pull the thread all the way through. **C D**

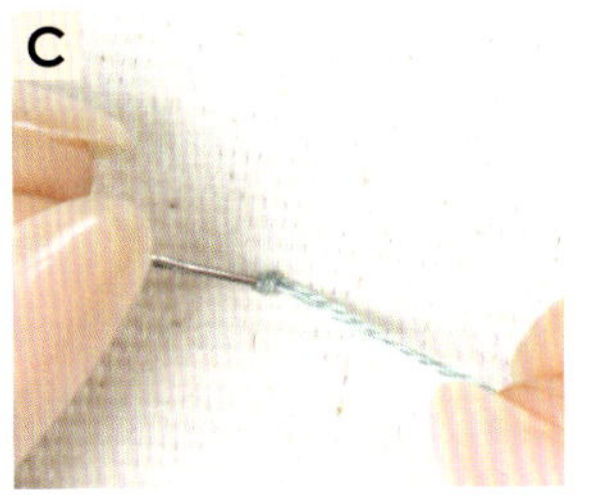
C

D

SEED STITCH

Seed stitches are typically used for filling and adding texture. I personally find them useful for integrating little accents of color and shading into tight corners.

1. Create a small straight stitch, and repeat as desired. **E**

E

STAB STITCH

Stab stitch is great for adding small dots of color to represent flowers or small leaves. It can also have a functional quality of holding down other stitches, an embroidery technique called *couching*.

1. Bring the needle up through the fabric, then insert it back down, catching just enough of the base fabric to create a tiny stitch on the surface, and repeat as desired. **F G**

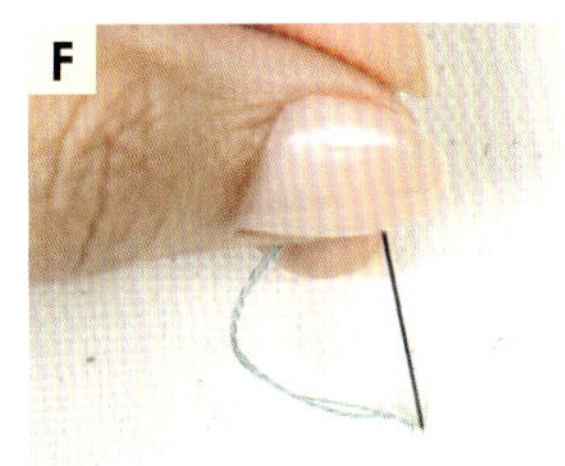
F

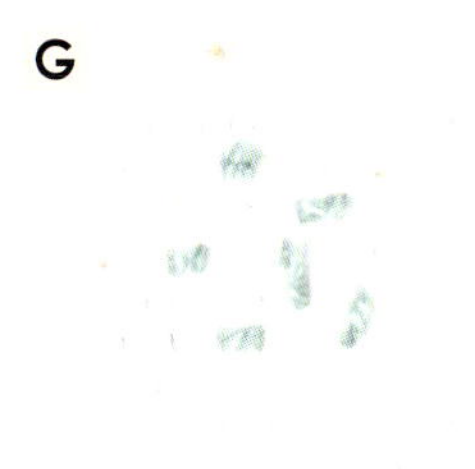
G

Landscape Element TUTORIALS

Because there are so many details in each element tutorial, each one comes with a Color Guide, and some include a Stitch Flow Guide. The color guides give you a visual breakdown of where each color is placed, which can be helpful in comparison to the blended colors in the step-by-step images. The stitch flow guides illustrate the stitch direction and movement of the stitching. This makes the stitch paths and directional changes clearer so you can successfully create realistic projects and elements. Refer to both guides as needed throughout the stitching process.

Each tutorial is pictured after being transferred to a 3″ (7.6cm) display hoop. Remember to reference the Stitch Library (page 26) for instructions on any unfamiliar stitches.

SKY & CLOUDS

The color transitions in stitching clouds are often so subtle that the stitch direction is what really helps to define the texture. Highlights and shadows also play a big part in making this element look realistic.

TOOLS & MATERIALS

- 5″ (12.7cm) embroidery hoop
- Tapestry needle, size 26
- Embroidery scissors
- Sky & Clouds Tutorial Pattern (page 154)
- 7″ × 7″ (17.8 × 17.8cm) square of natural-colored cotton duck canvas
- DMC six-stranded cotton embroidery floss (colors below)

DMC THREAD COLORS

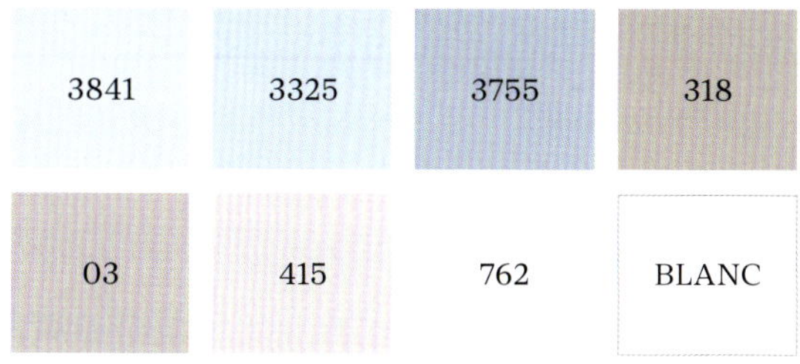

STITCHES USED

Long and Short Stitch, page 28

Straight Stitch, page 27

Seed Stitch, page 29

Split Back Stitch, page 28

Satin Stitch, page 28

COLOR GUIDE

TRANSFERRING THE PATTERN

Transfer the design onto the center of the 7″ × 7″ (17.8 × 17.8cm) fabric square (see Transferring Designs, page 17). Secure the fabric in the 5″ (12.7cm) hoop.

STITCHING

Use 2 strands of thread unless otherwise noted.

Sky

1. Use horizontal long and short stitches of 3841 to fill the section below the cloud. **A**

2. Stitch 2–3 straight stitches of 3841 in the lower half of the middle section on both sides. Then, blend long and short stitches of 3325 to fill the section. Blend 3325 with the bottom section. Stitch 3–5 straight stitches of 3325 to the lower half of the top section. **B**

A

B

3. Use a combination of long and short stitches and seed stitches to fill the top section with 3755. Blend 3755 with the middle section. C D

Creating A Gradient

Loosely blending straight stitches of one color into existing stitches of another color helps create a gradual gradient.

Cloud: Left

1. Use a combination of slightly curved long and short stitches and seed stitches in 318 to shade the section in the bottom left of the cloud. E

2. Use 03 to blend stitches around the stitches from Step 1. Fill the small area above with seed stitches of the same color. F

3. With small split back stitches of 03, line the border above the Step 1 section. Shade the central section with 03 satin stitches. G

4. Fill the bottom left corner with long and short stitches of 415. Angle overlapping seed stitches of the same color, making sure to leave 2 spaces for the next colors. H

5. Use small split back stitches of 415 to shade above the 03 stitches from Step 2. Angle seed stitches up the shape. I

6. Line the bottom border of the cloud with 762, overlapping split back stitches and straight stitches. Fill the right open space from Step 4 with the same color. J

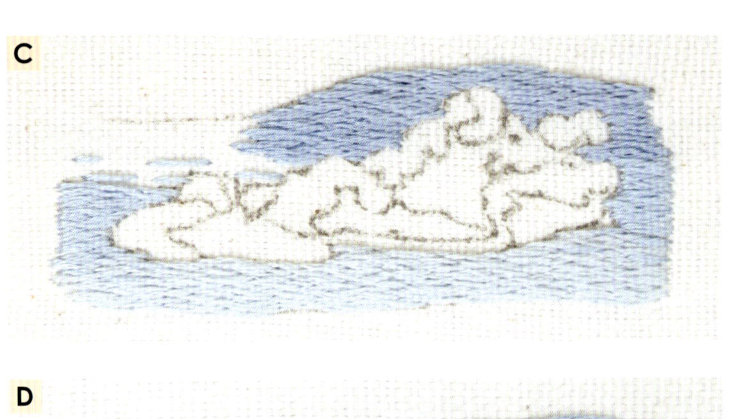

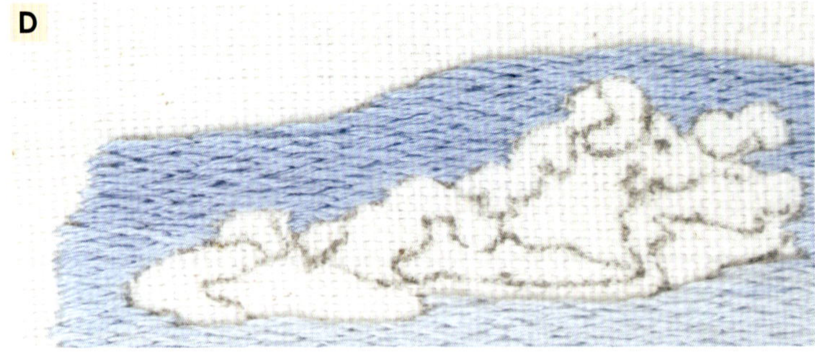

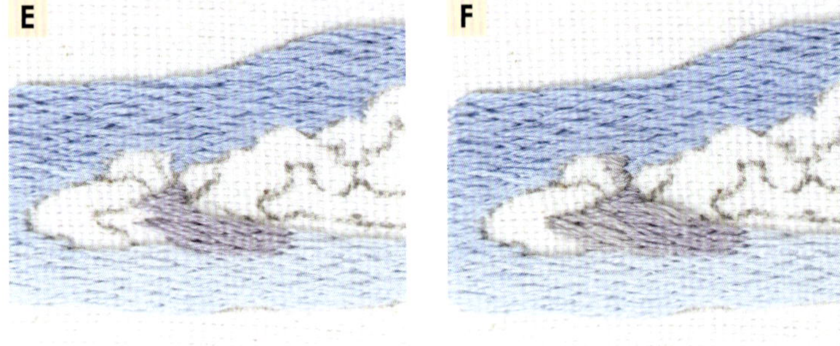

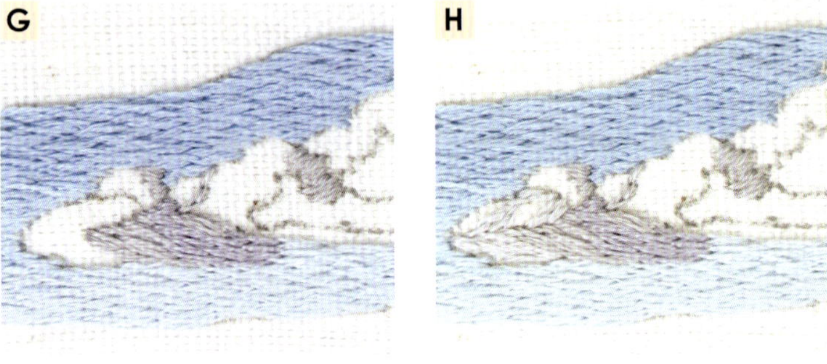

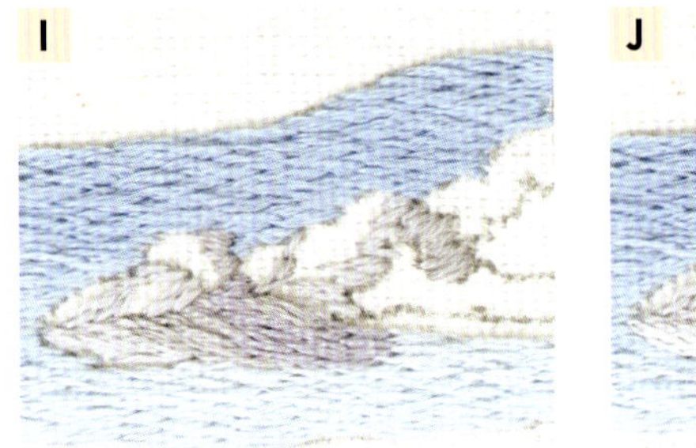

7. Blend a few 762 seed stitches into the small open areas near the top border. Blend 762 with the Step 5 stitches. Stitch angled seed stitches with the same color to continue the gradient. **K**

8. Use a combination of overlapping BLANC seed stitches and long and short stitches to fill in the 4 remaining open spaces on the left side. **L**

Cloud: Right

1. Fill the large area near the center of the cloud with long and short stitches of 318. Repeat on the right side of the cloud. **A**

2. Use 03 to blend long and short stitches into the large space between the 2 patches of 318, noting the stitch direction. **B**

3. Fill the bottom right corner of the cloud with 03. Add seed stitches in and to the right of the 318 patch above. **C**

4. Sweep 415 long and short stitches along the bottom border. Fill the right side of the top cloud bump with the same color. **D**

5. Add seed stitches of 415 to the left and middle of the Step 2 section. Fill the far right section with 415 long and short stitches, leaving 2 spaces for the next color. **E**

6. Blend 762 seed stitches into the central open area and top right section. Fill the remaining spaces in the bottom half of the cloud with the same color. **F**

7. With small, overlapping BLANC seed stitches, fill the remaining open space along the top border. Add 3841 seed and straight stitches as accents. **G**

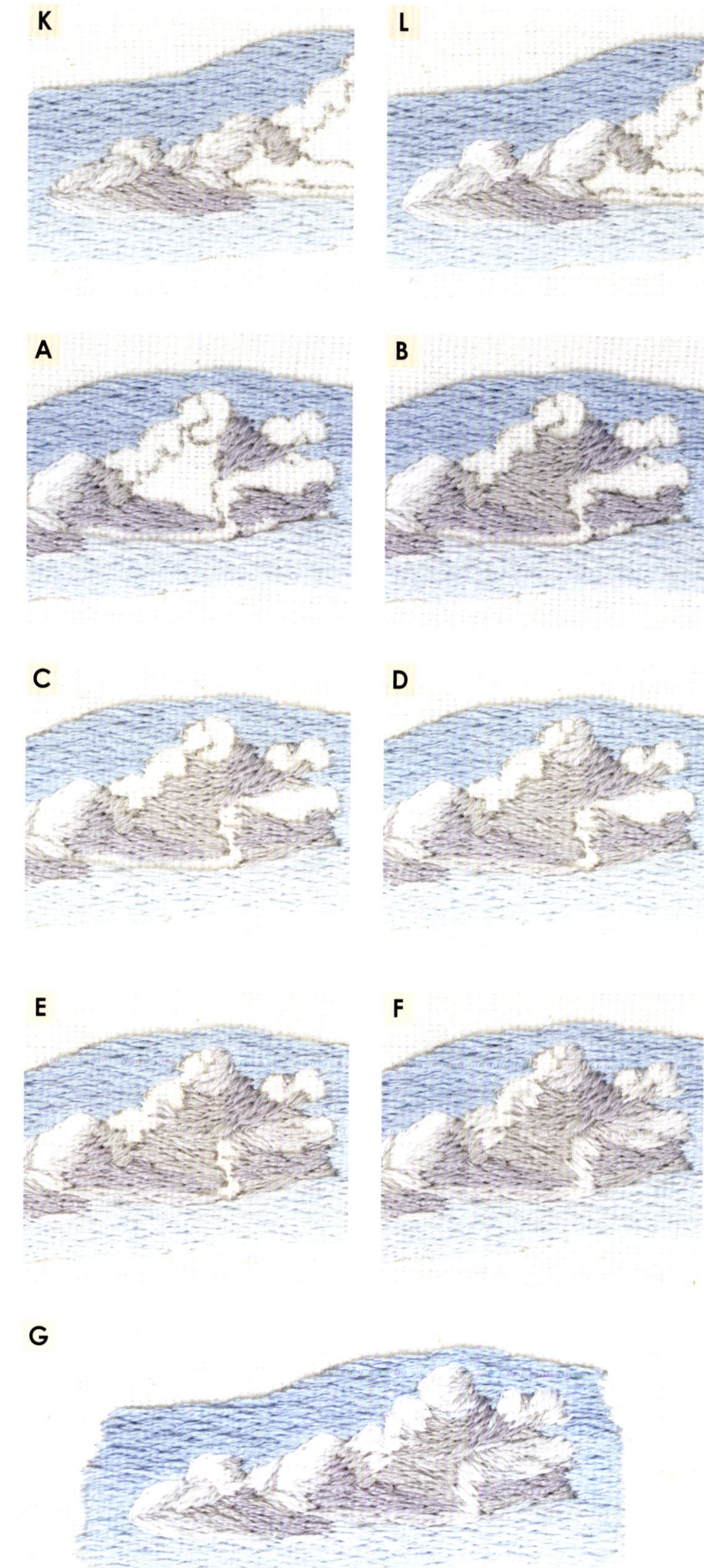

HILLS

It may be tempting to make all your stitches flow in the same downward direction when creating a hill, but hills have lots of swells and depressions! Varying the stitch direction adds texture to the terrain, and accentuating the highlights and shadows will make this element seem more lifelike.

TOOLS & MATERIALS

- 5″ (12.7cm) embroidery hoop
- Tapestry needle, size 26
- Embroidery scissors
- Hills Tutorial Pattern (page 154)
- 7″ × 7″ (17.8 × 17.8cm) square of natural-colored cotton duck canvas
- DMC six-stranded cotton embroidery floss (colors below)

DMC THREAD COLORS

STITCHES USED

Satin Stitch, page 28

Seed Stitch, page 29

Split Back Stitch, page 28

Long and Short Stitch, page 28

Straight Stitch, page 27

COLOR GUIDE

STITCH FLOW GUIDE

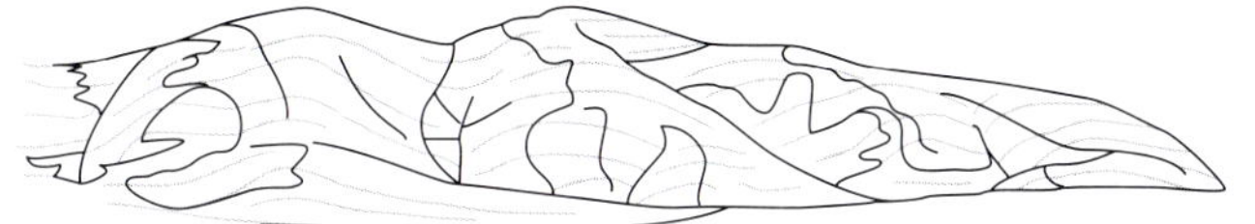

TRANSFERRING THE PATTERN

Transfer the design onto the center of the 7″ × 7″ (17.8 × 17.8cm) fabric square (see Transferring Designs, page 17). Secure the fabric in the 5″ (12.7cm) hoop.

STITCHING

Use 2 strands of thread unless otherwise noted.

Right Hill

1. Shade the far right section with 3750 satin stitches. Fill the central section with 3750 seed and satin stitches. Add 924 split back stitches along the top border. A

A

2. Blend in 924 long and short stitches and seed stitches. B

Single Stitches

Single stitches of a color might seem unnecessary, but when you're thread painting on such a small scale, they are essential in creating a smooth color transition.

3. Blend in 501 seed stitches and long and short stitches, filling in the curved shapes. Add 502 seed stitches to fill along the bottom border. C

4. Blend in seed stitches of 3362. Use a combination of 3012 seed stitches and long and short stitches to fill in more of the hill (referring to the Color Guide). D

5. Blend in 4 seed stitches of 3045. Then, fill in a section of the same color at the bottom. E

6. Use 3046 seed stitches to fill in the remaining space on the right side of the hill, blending and rounding the curves per the Stitch Flow Guide (see Creating Movement, page 20). F

7. Add 2 straight stitches with 1 strand of 3047 along the top border of the hill. Split back stitch in the bottom right for another highlight. G

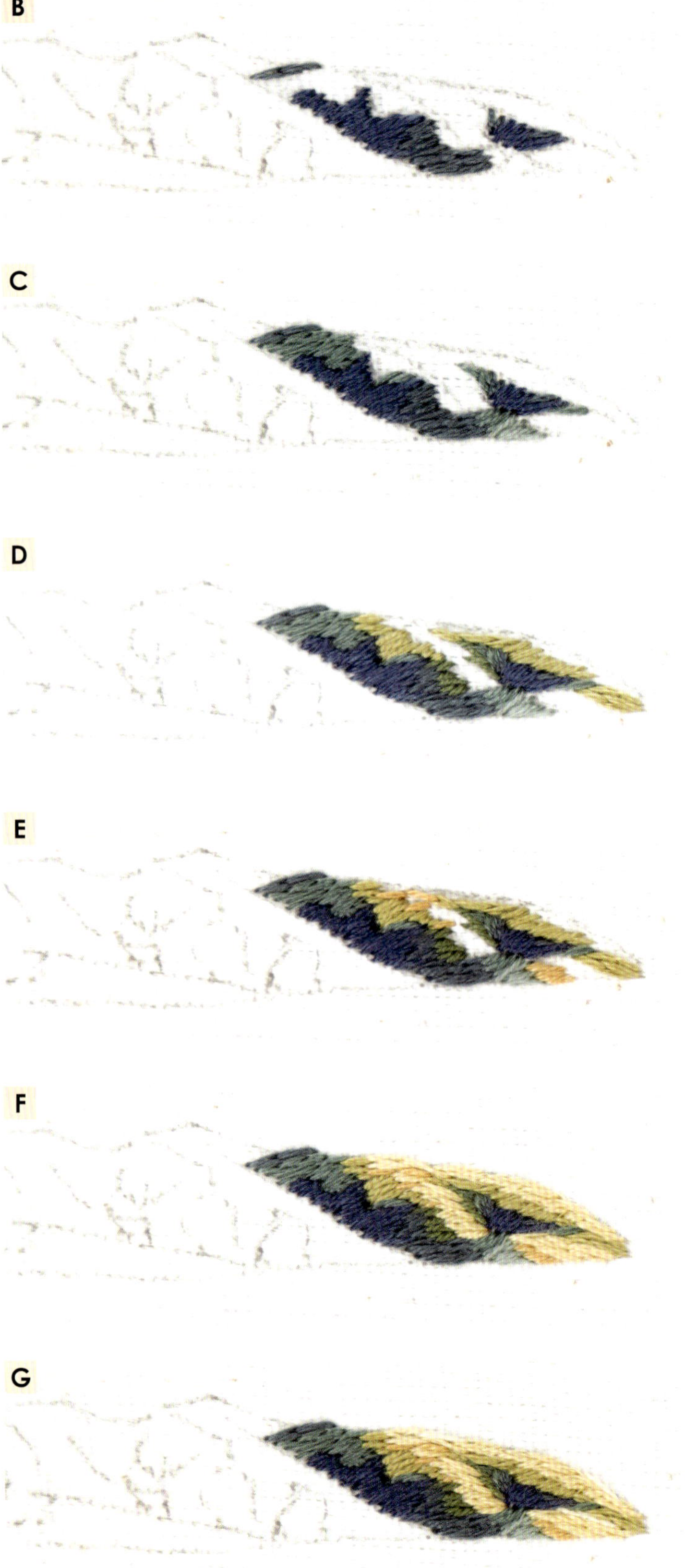

Middle Hill

1. Seed stitch 3750 in a *V*-shape. Fill the 2 other sections with satin stitches in the same color. **A**

2. Use slanted 924 satin stitches to shade above the *V*. Blend the same color with the right section. **B**

3. With overlapping 501 seed stitches, shade around the 924 stitch areas. **C**

4. Use 502 seed and satin stitches to fill below both sides of the *V*. **D**

5. Blend in 3362 long and short stitches to the central section. Add seed stitches and satin stitches of the same color to the right section. **E**

6. Add 3045 seed and satin stitches. Fill the space between the 2 sections with long and short stitches of 3012. Repeat at the top border. **F G**

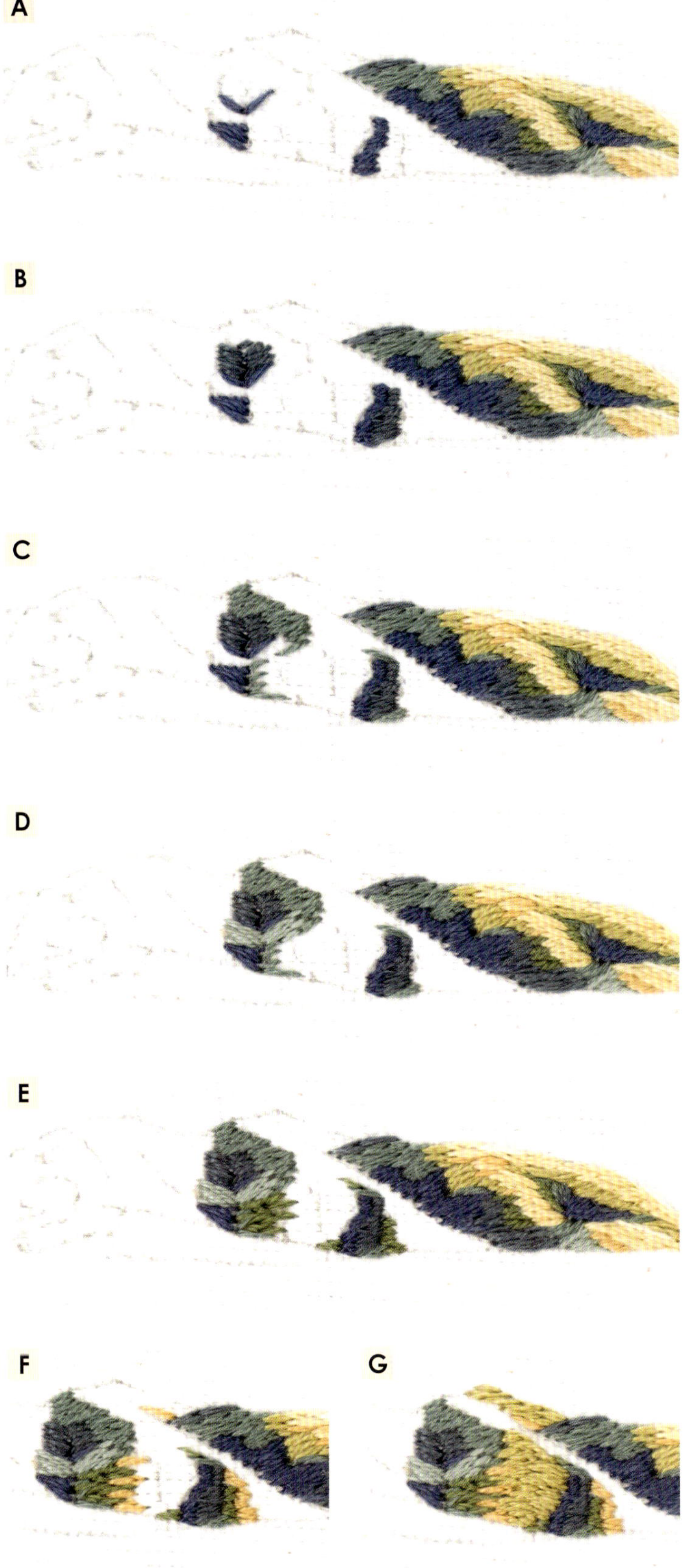

7. Seed stitch 3012 at the top of the hill. Blend long and short stitches of the same color at the bottom of the section. **H**

8. Fill the remaining border with long and short stitches of 3046. **I**

9. With 1 strand of 3047, split back stitch along the right border of the hill. Seed stitch at the top. **J**

Left Hill

1. Add 924 satin and seed stitches in the left section. Add 501 long and short stitches and satin stitches in the right section. Blend 501 seed stitches into the left side of the 924 section. **A**

2. Blend in 3362 long and short stitches and seed stitches. **B**

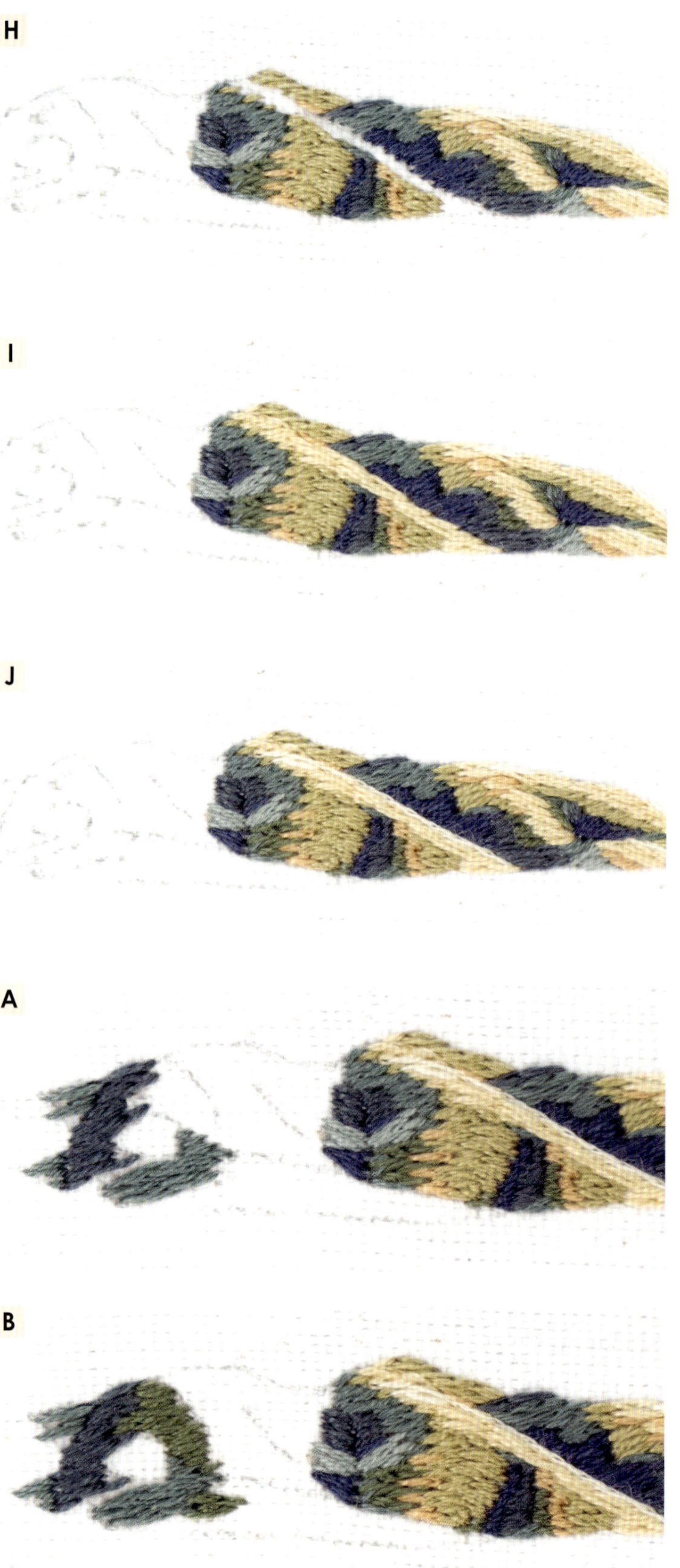

3. Add 3012 long and short stitches near the bottom of the hill. Add 2 seed stitches at the top and bottom. **C**

4. Blend in 3045 seed stitches, leaving a small gap in the circular area. **D**

5. Sweep slanted 3045 long and short stitches along the right side of the hill. Fill in the bottom of the hill with the same stitching. **E**

6. Blend 3046 seed stitches and long and short stitches into the remaining areas, making sure to curve along with the Stitch Flow Guide. **F**

7. With 1 strand of 3047, add 1 straight stitch to the top of the hill. Split back stitch the slope near the center bottom. **G**

C

D

E

F

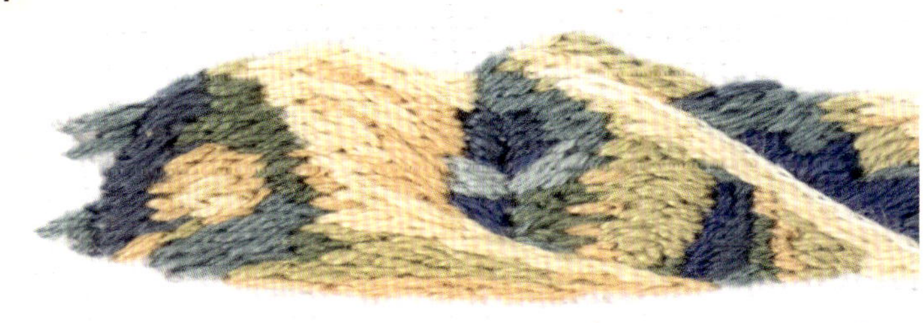

G

MOUNTAINS

While similar to hills, mountains have peaks and crevices defined by much straighter lines. The addition of this element in a landscape thread painting can create a focal point that establishes a sense of balance in the scene.

TOOLS & MATERIALS

- 5″ (12.7cm) embroidery hoop
- Tapestry needle, size 26
- Embroidery scissors
- Mountains Tutorial Pattern (page 155)
- 7″ × 7″ (17.8 × 17.8cm) square of natural-colored cotton duck canvas
- DMC six-stranded cotton embroidery floss (colors below)

DMC THREAD COLORS

STITCHES USED

Long and Short Stitch, page 28

Seed Stitch, page 29

Satin Stitch, page 28

Stab Stitch, page 29

Split Back Stitch, page 28

Straight Stitch, page 27

COLOR GUIDE

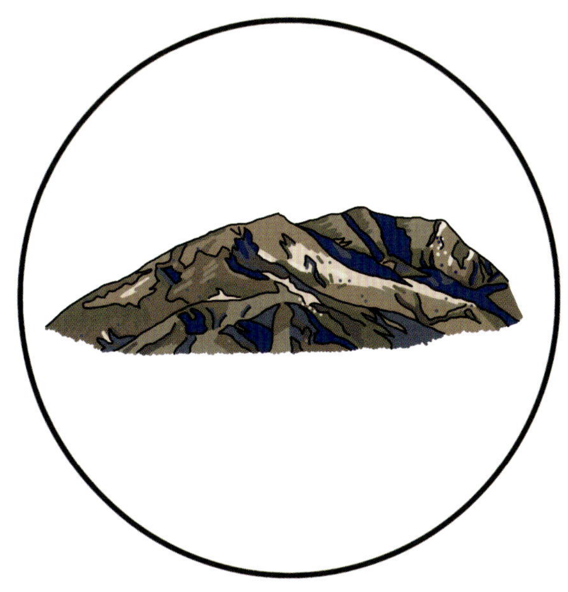

TRANSFERRING THE PATTERN

Transfer the design onto the center of the 7″ × 7″ (17.8 × 17.8cm) fabric square (see Transferring Designs, page 17). Secure the fabric in the 5″ (12.7cm) hoop.

STITCHING

Use 2 strands of thread unless otherwise noted.

Right Range

1. Use long and short stitches and seed stitches of 336 to fill in the 4 sections on the right side of the mountain. **A**

2. Blend in seed stitches of 930. Then, blend in seed stitches of 413. **B**

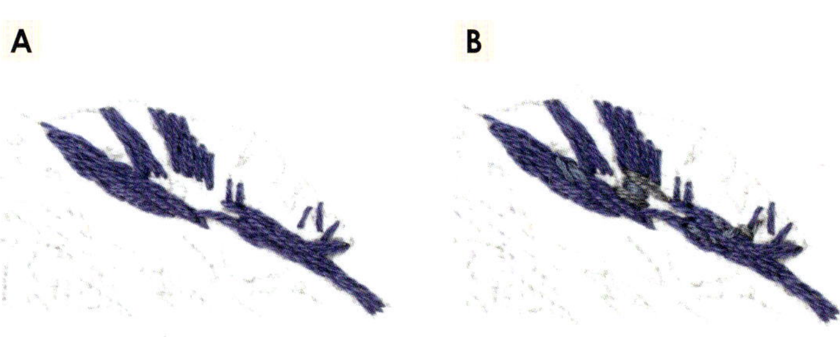

3. Add perpendicular seed stitches of 535 at the top border, then blend it between the 336 sections. Blend in satin stitches and seed stitches of the same color near the bottom right. C

4. Fill in 645 seed stitches and long and short stitches in the bottom right corner. D

5. Use long and short stitches of 646 to fill the open space at the top between the 336 sections. E

6. Fill the remaining open space with long and short stitches and seed stitches of 07. F

Layering Accent Stitches

Adding stab and seed stitches for highlights and shadows after you have laid down the base colors helps to build the texture of the rock face.

7. Seed stitch highlights with 1 strand of 3033. Layer stab stitches of the same color. With 1 strand of 336, add several stab stitches. G

Peak Midsection

1. Use a combination of 336 long and short stitches, satin stitches, and seed stitches to create the deepest shadows. A

2. Blend in and add 930 seed stitches. B

3. Blend in 413 long and short stitches and seed stitches across the mountain. C D

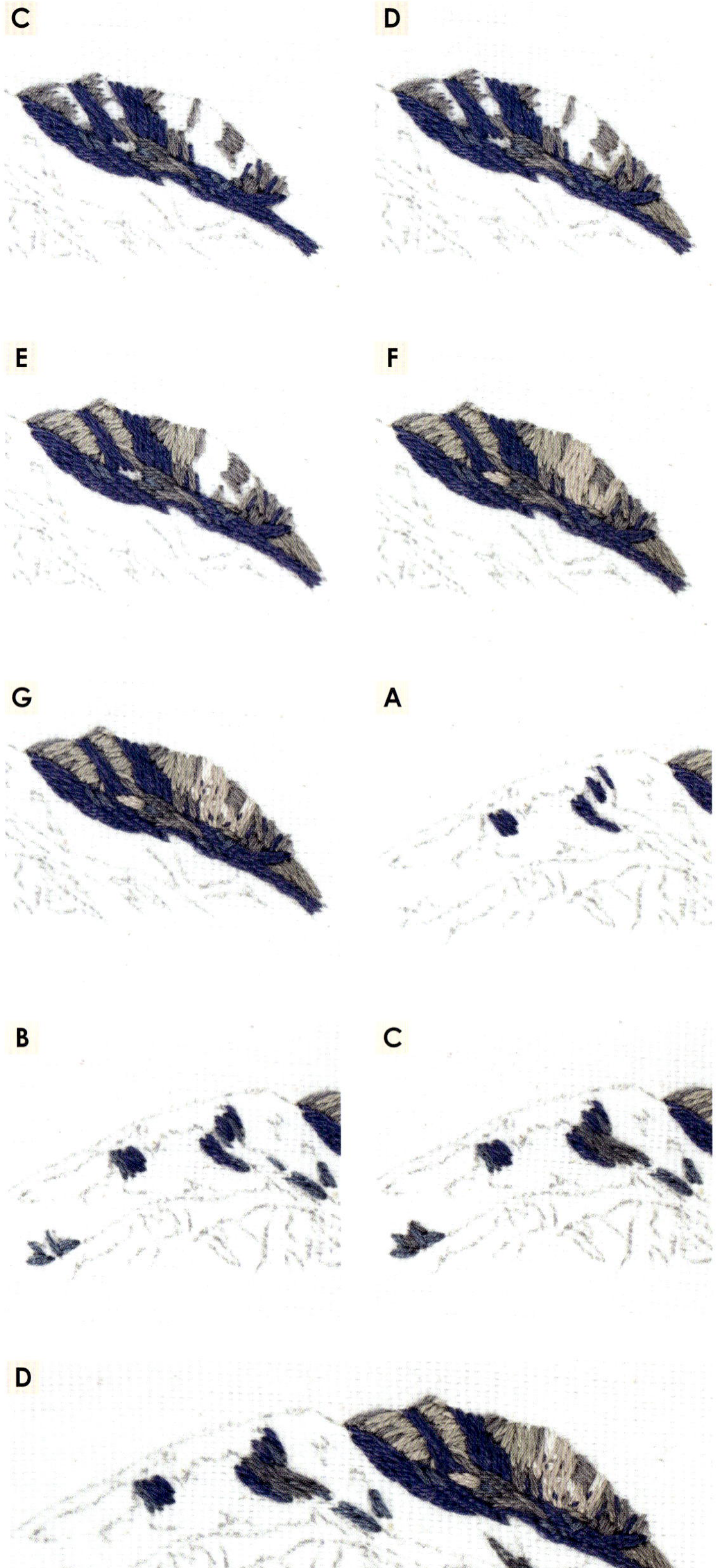

4. Blend in overlapping 535 seed stitches. Add split back stitches to the top border. Fan out a combination of long and short stitches and seed stitches to shade the bottom left. E

5. Shade the lower right with 535 seed stitches and long and short stitches. F

6. Add long and short stitches of 645 to fill in the open spaces between color sections, paying attention to stitch direction. G

7. Split back stitch with 646 along the left border. Layer accent seed stitches into the section from Step 6. H

8. Blend a combination of slanted 646 straight stitches and seed stitches with the stitches on the right. I

9. Blend 07 long and short stitches up towards the peak of the mountain. Slant long and short stitches of the same color to shade the top portion of the slope and above the foothills. J

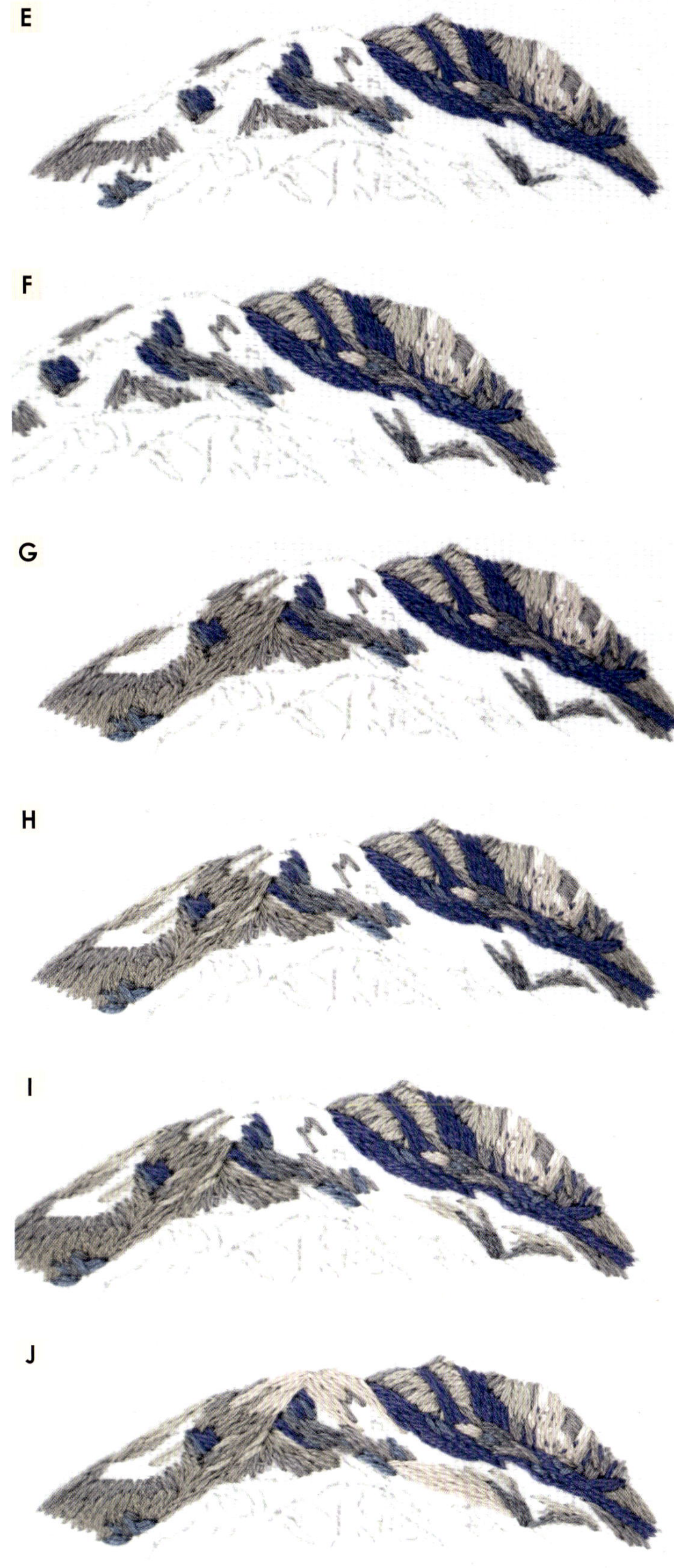

10. With 07 long and short stitches, shade around the stitches to the right. K

11. Use 07 long and short stitches to fill the left, leaving a small space for the next color. Add accent seed stitches of the same color to the right. L

12. Fill the remaining space on the left with 06 long and short stitches. Add 1 small seed stitch of the same color to the 930 stitches below. M

13. Fill the central and right areas with long and short 06 stitches. N

14. Use 1 strand of 930 to blend 4 or 5 seed stitches into the upper right side of the mountain. Sprinkle stab stitches of the same color down the slope. O

15. With 1 strand of 535, layer small seed stitches on the right slope. With 1 strand of 3033, blend 3 or 4 stab stitches along the bottom of the long 06 patch. Use 1 strand of 930 to add stab stitches on the left slope. P

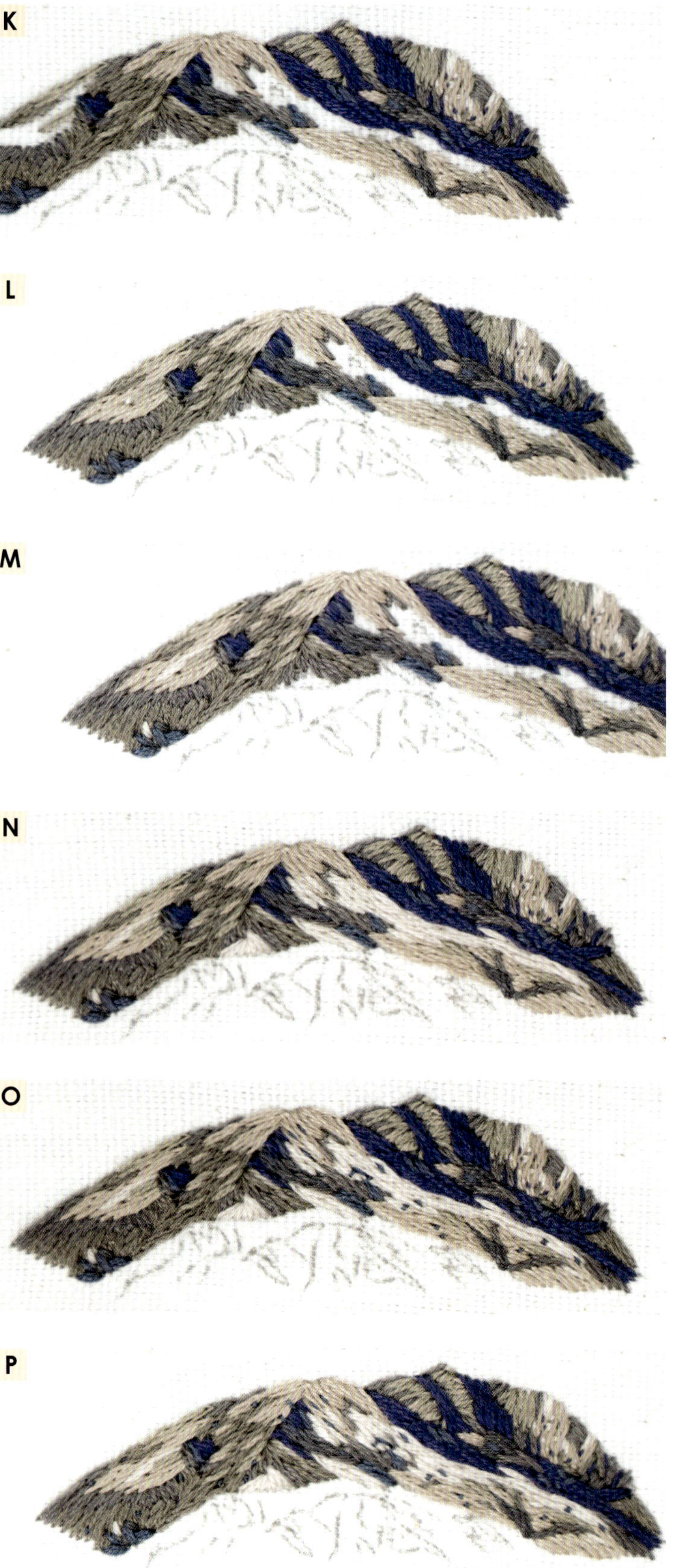

Foothills

1. Shade 3 sections with 336 long and short stitches. **A**

2. Blend in a combination of 930 seed stitches and satin stitches. Create a new section of the same color with long and short stitches on the right. **B**

3. Shade the left side with 413 long and short stitches and seed stitches. Blend in the middle and right with the same color. **C**

4. Blend in long and short stitches of 535. **D**

5. Tuck in 645 seed stitches near the Step 2 stitches. Add satin stitches to the middle. Fill the right side with seed stitches and long and short stitches. **E**

6. Fill the left corner with long and short stitches of 646. Add seed stitches to the top border of the foothills, then fill in the remaining open space with a combination of satin stitches and seed stitches. **F**

7. Use 1 strand of 07 to add stab stitches across the left side. Use 1 strand of 06 to add 4 or 5 stab stitches to line the top right border. **G**

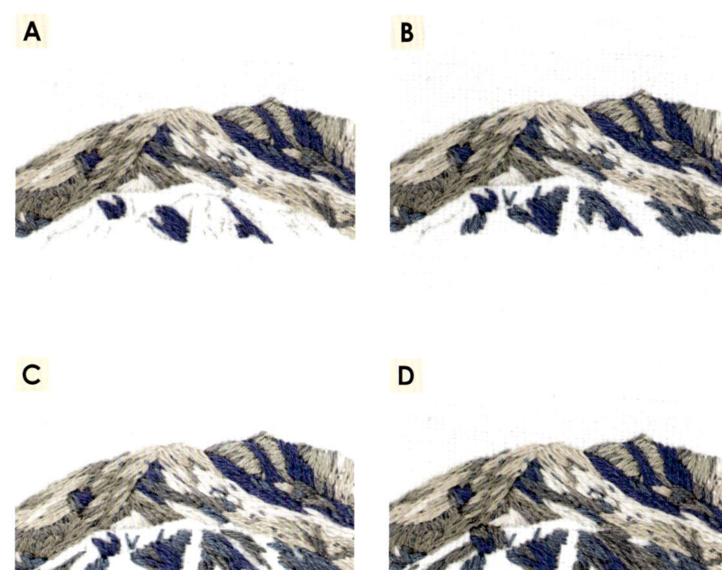

TREE

In nature, trees come in so many shapes, sizes, and colors, so there are quite a few ways you can stitch them. My favorite way to adorn a tree is with clusters of French knots. As you gradually build texture with the knots, you'll love watching the tree slowly come alive with each layer of color.

TOOLS & MATERIALS

- 5″ (12.7cm) embroidery hoop
- Tapestry needle, size 26
- Embroidery scissors
- Tree Tutorial Pattern (page 155)
- Hoop stand (recommended)
- 7″ × 7″ (17.8 × 17.8cm) square of natural-colored cotton duck canvas
- DMC six-stranded cotton embroidery floss (colors below)

DMC THREAD COLORS

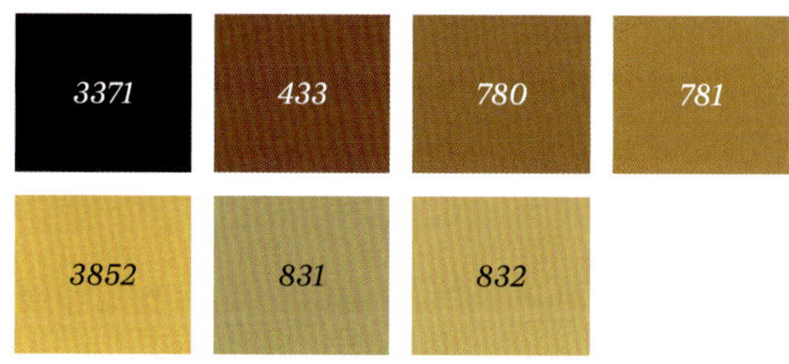

STITCHES USED

Long and Short Stitch, page 28

Split Back Stitch, page 28

French Knot, page 29

Seed Stitch, page 29

COLOR GUIDE

TRANSFERRING THE PATTERN

Transfer the design onto the center of the 7″ × 7″ (17.8 × 17.8cm) fabric square (see Transferring Designs, page 17). Secure the fabric in the 5″ (12.7cm) hoop.

STITCHING

Use 2 strands of thread unless otherwise noted. Make single-loop French knots any time French knots or knots are referenced.

Hoop Stand

I recommend using a hoop stand for projects with heavy French knot work. It takes the strain off your fingers and wrists and makes creating this decorative stitch a whole lot easier.

Trunk and Branches

1. Long and short stitch the trunk with 3371. Split back stitch the thicker branches. A

2. With 1 strand of 3371, split back stitch the thinner branches to complete the skeleton of the tree. B

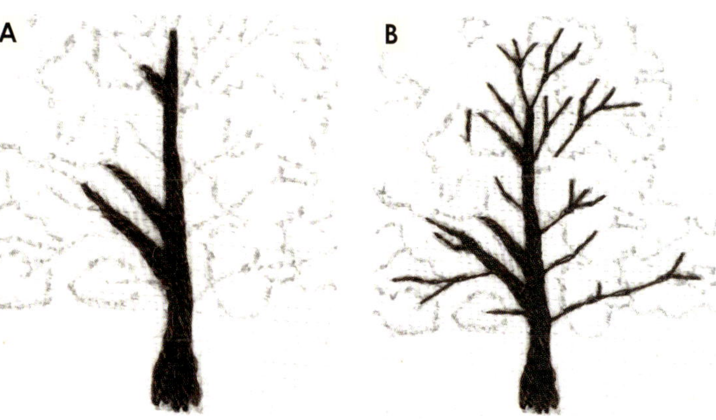

Foliage: Left Side

1. With 433 French knots, fill in sections at the bottom left of the tree. A

2. Loosely fill the area below the highest cluster with 433 French knots. Repeat above the cluster. B

Leaving Space

Leaving gaps between the knots of the foliage will allow some of the background to show through, which makes a more realistic tree.

3. Add several more clusters of 433 French knots up the left side of the tree. Add more knots between the branches and trunk. Refer to the Color Guide to see where the gaps in the foliage should be. C

4. Begin filling some of the open space in the bottom left with French knots in 780. Leave a round gap in the bottom left branch. Blend and disperse knots up the center left of the tree. D

5. Continue blending 780 knots up to the trunk, careful not to cover the branches. Add 2 seed stitches in 781 around the thin bottom left branch. E

Seed Stitch

Seed stitches come in handy when you want to add color near thin branches, and French knots are too large and will most likely cover them. Add them parallel to the thin branches, or tuck a couple into corners where multiple branches meet.

6. Blend 781 French knots to fill the remainder of the bottom left foliage. Blend them in the central left area. Add 1 or 2 accent knots slightly outside of the section to represent stray leaves. Layer heavily, building up the dimension of the tree and covering the tips of the twigs. Add a seed stitch next to the thin branches if necessary. F

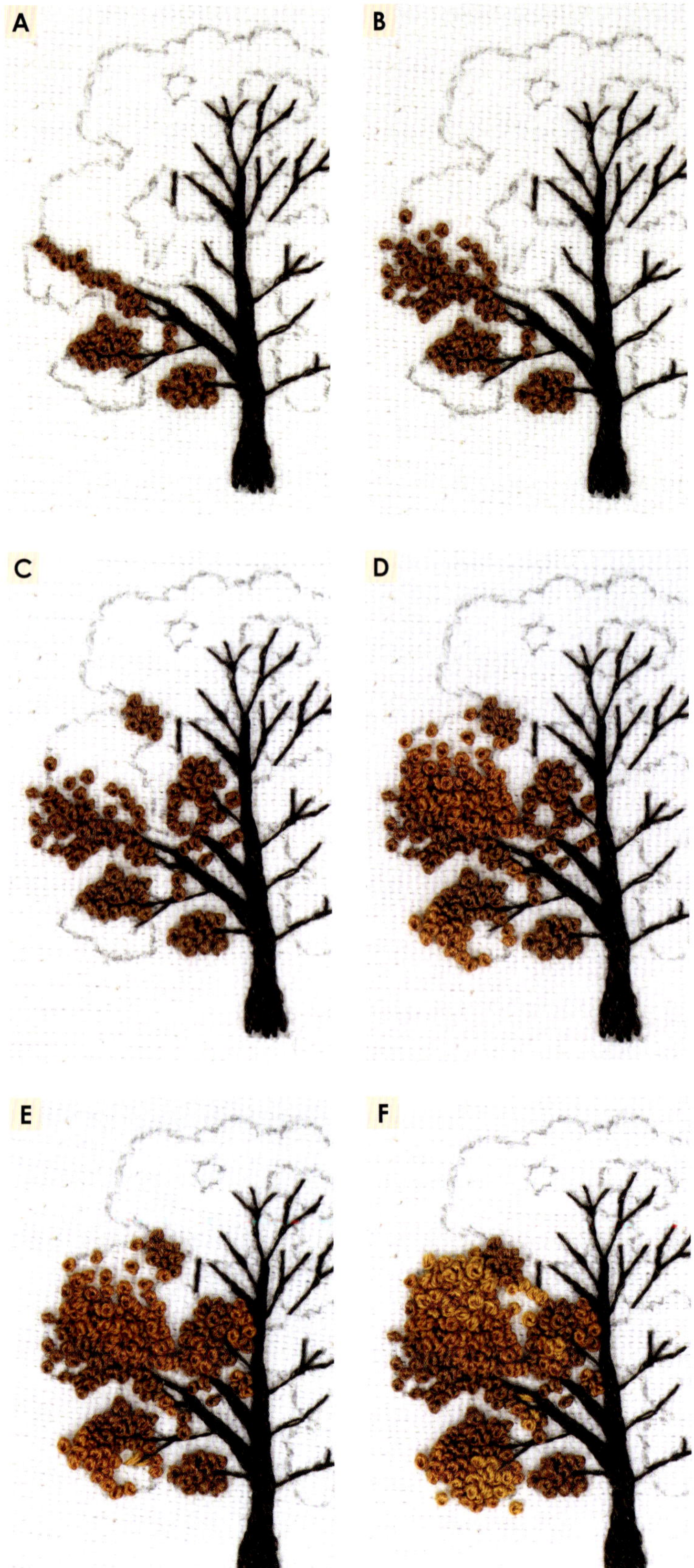

7. Fill in the final remaining section on the left with knots of 3852, again building dimension. Cover the tip of the thin branch at the bottom left with one knot. G

Foliage: Top

1. Fill in large swathes of the top of the tree with French knots of 433. Add 2 seed stitches in the *V* of thin branches at the top. Leave small gaps for other colors as indicated by the Color Guide. A

2. Blend in French knots of 780 into the existing knots, moving from the top of the tree toward the branches. B

3. Add more 780 knots moving toward the right, blending them into the thin branches with seed stitches as needed. C

4. Add more 780 French knots toward the top right of the tree, following the shape of the Color Guide. Add clusters moving down the right side. Nestle a seed stitch between the thin branches. D

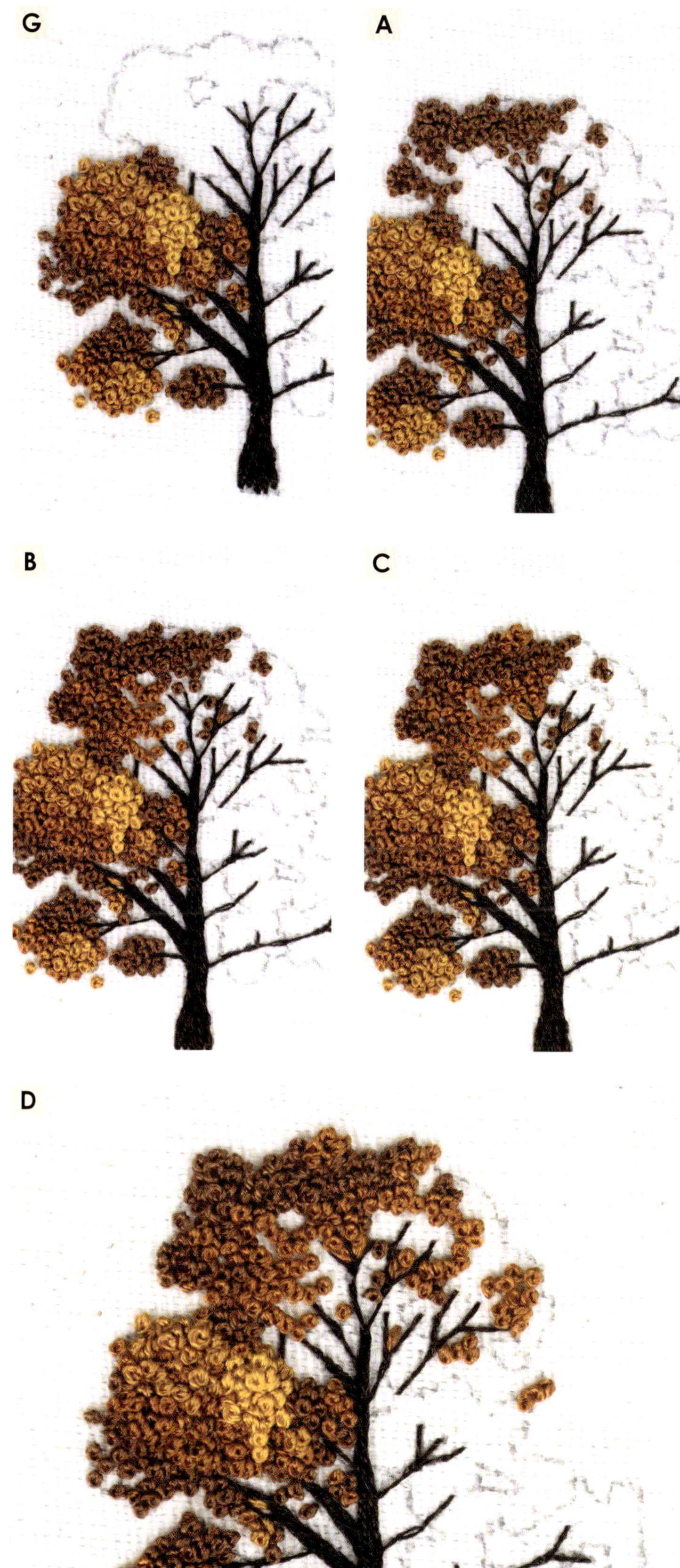

5. Add French knots in 781 to blend in on the top of the tree. E F

6. Continue blending in 781 French knots and seed stitches moving down the right side of the tree. G

7. Use a combination of dense French knots and seed stitches in 3852 to fill the remaining open spaces at the top of the tree (remembering to leave gaps as indicated by the Color Guide). H

Foliage: Right Side

1. Add clusters and accent French knots of 433 in the bottom right of the tree. A

2. Blend in clusters and accents of 780 French knots. Make sure not to cover the thin branches as you shade. B

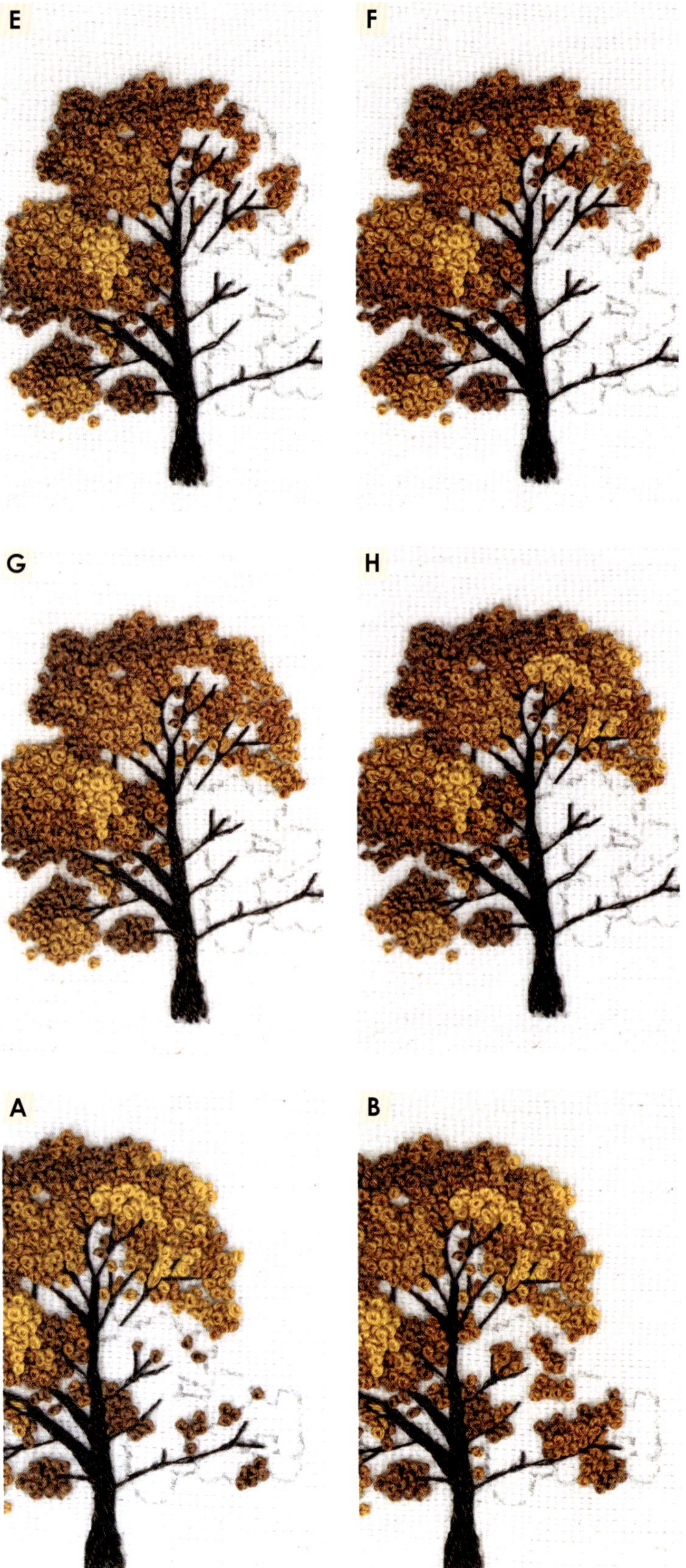

3. Add more accents with 780 knots along the right side. **C**

4. Blend in 781 French knots up the right side near the trunk. Heavily layer the knots in the central area around the pronged branch, allowing a knot or 2 to partially cover the trunk to accentuate the roundness of the foliage patch. **D**

5. Fill in more 781 French knots along the right border of the tree, densely covering the space. **E**

6. Densely fill the remaining open space up the center of the section with 3852 knots. Add accent knots throughout the foliage at the far right. **F**

7. Partially fill the remaining open space at the bottom with 831 French knots. **G**

8. Heavily layer 832 knots to fill the remaining space. Add 1 accent knot to the right. **H**

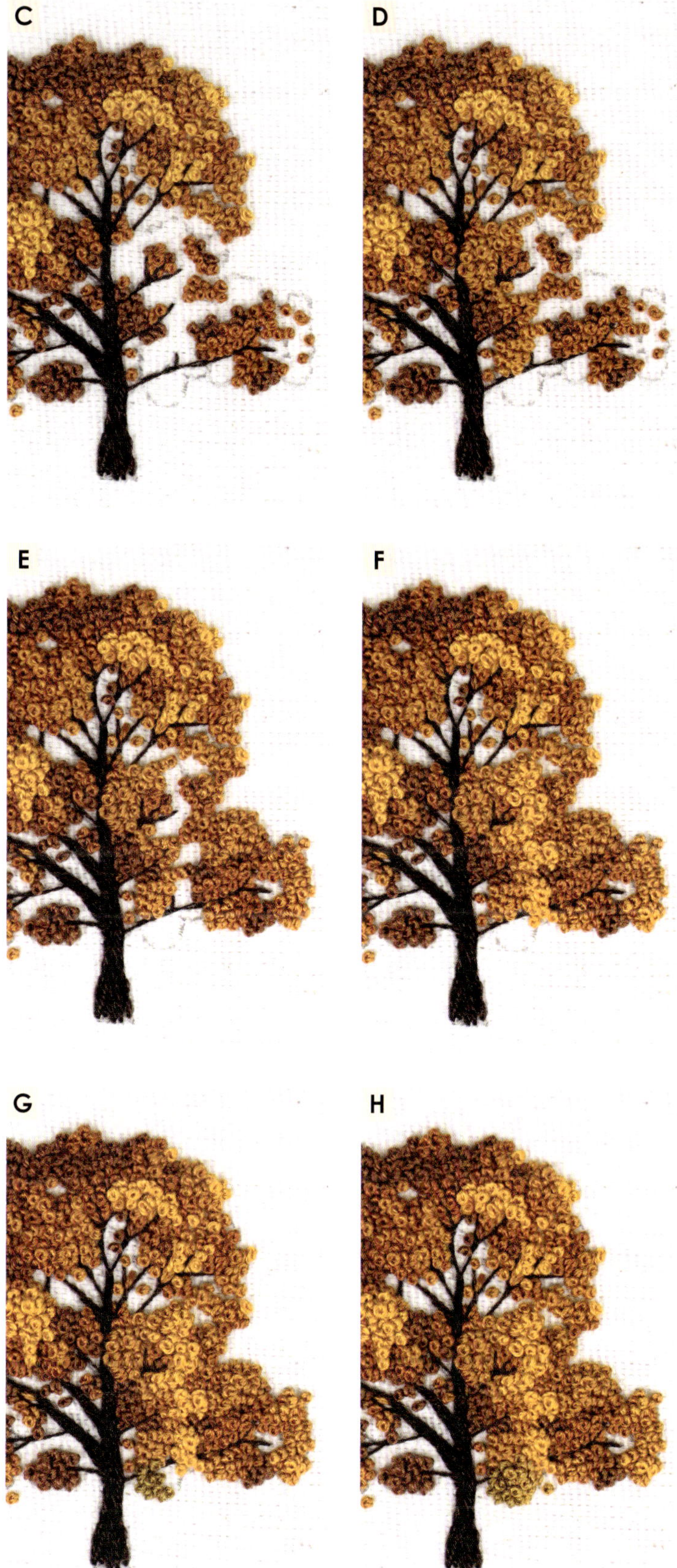

GRASS

Embroidering grass in a landscape thread painting is all about layering and creating subtle differences in the angles of your stitches. Gradually layering lighter blades over the darker ones will give a perception of depth. Adding curves to the stems creates a sense of movement in the scene's environment.

TOOLS & MATERIALS

- 5″ (12.7cm) embroidery hoop
- Tapestry needle, size 26
- Embroidery scissors
- Grass Tutorial Pattern (page 155)
- 7″ × 7″ (17.8 × 17.8cm) square of natural-colored cotton duck canvas
- DMC six-stranded cotton embroidery floss (colors below)

DMC THREAD COLORS

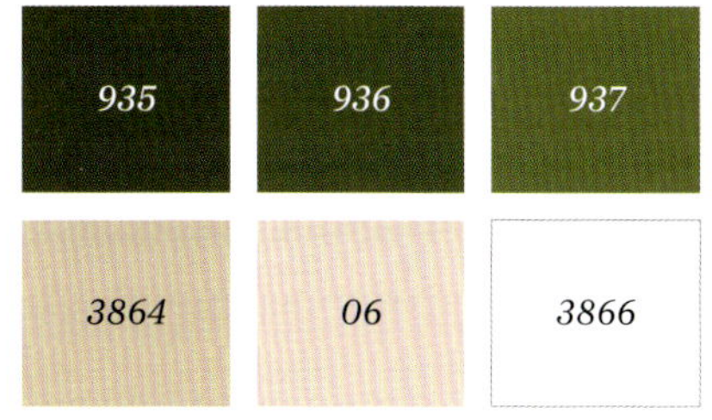

STITCHES USED

Split Back Stitch, page 28

Straight Stitch, page 27

Seed Stitch, page 29

COLOR GUIDE

TRANSFERRING THE PATTERN

Transfer the design onto the center of the 7″ × 7″ (17.8 × 17.8cm) fabric square (see Transferring Designs, page 17). Secure the fabric in the 5″ (12.7cm) hoop.

STITCHING

Use 2 strands of thread unless otherwise noted.

Base

1. Split back stitch in 935 to create the first layer of grass. Start at the base and stitch up, varying the height of each stem. A B

Losing Guidelines Behind Stitches

When stitching this pattern, some of the guidelines will get lost as you work your way upward. Keeping a photo of the pattern nearby can help you recall where stitches should be placed.

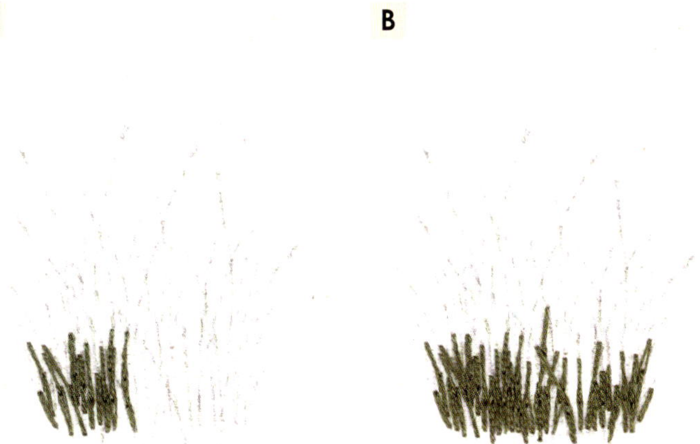

2. Blend 936 split back stitches into the 935 stitches from the previous step, giving more length to the stems. C D

Keeping Track of Layers

To avoid the grass taking on a flat, 2-dimensional appearance, it's important to keep track of the blades that you want to remain in the foreground. Be consistent with the placement of their stitches, and layer them on top of those in the background.

3. Add 4 long straight stitches of 936 that shoot up from the base and overlap the 935 stitches. E

Midsection Stems

1. Blend 937 split back stitches down into the ends of the upper 936 stitches, leaving space at the tops of most of the stems for the next color. Continue across the section, keeping the taller stems in the background. A

2. Fill in more of the middle gaps with 937, placing 1–2 straight stitches between the 936 stems. Layer 3 long straight stitches of 937 from the base. B

3. Always use 1 strand of 3864. Complete the longest 937 stems with split back stitches of 3864. At the end of each shorter 937 stem, add 1 small straight stitch in 3864. Make sure to keep track of background and foreground stems so you can overlap them accordingly. C

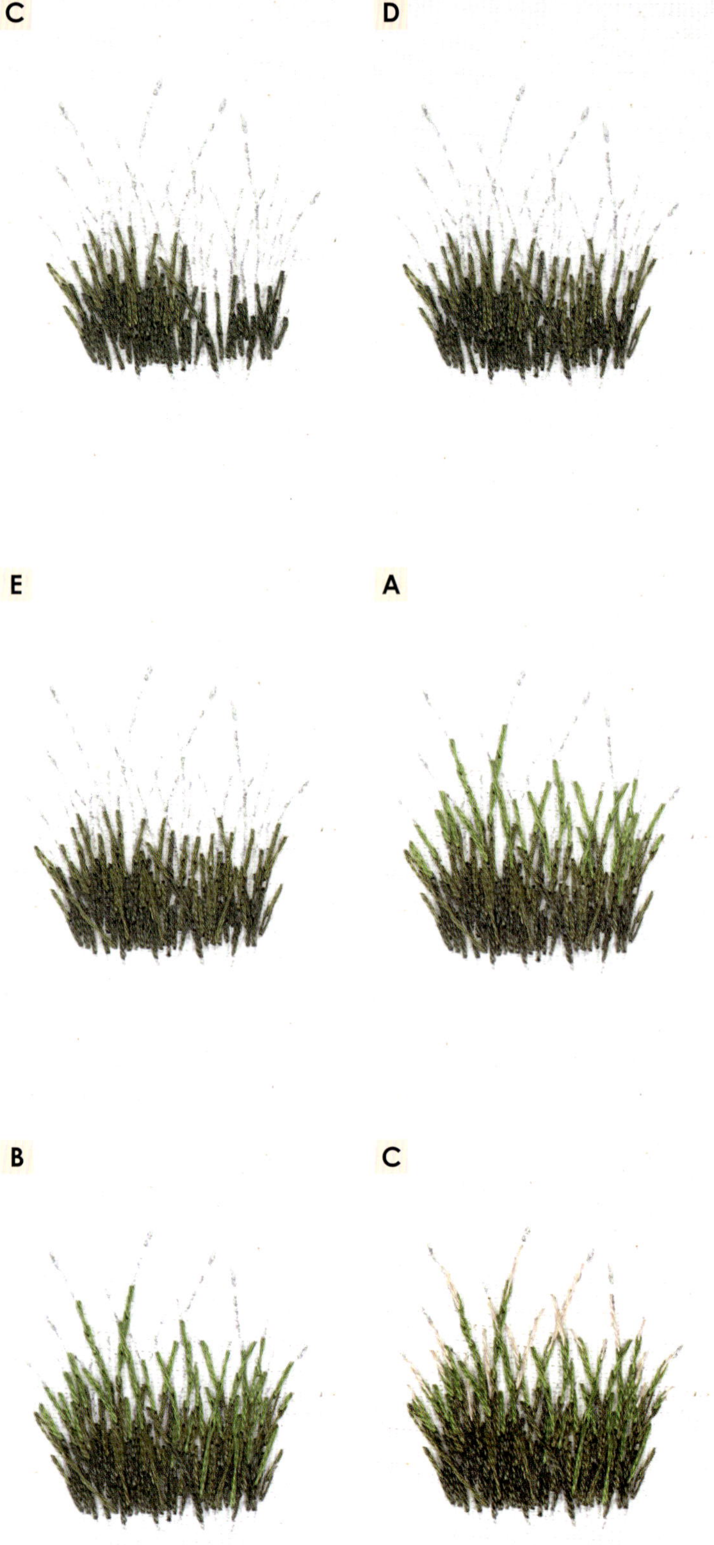

4. Add angled straight stitches of 3864 between the 937 and 936 stems. Fan stitches of the same color up toward the taller stems, making sure not to cover any of the existing green stitches. D

5. Add 3864 straight stitches and seed stitches in any open spaces down to the base of the grass. E

6. Use 3864 split back stitches to create 3 curved stems in the foreground on the right. F

Upper Blades

Use 1 strand for this entire section.

1. Shade the 4 tallest stems (that include the unstitched seed heads) with 06 straight stitches. Fill in the remaining upper areas with more 06 stitches. A

2. Split back stitch 06 to create tall stems at the top that fan outward. B

3. Overlap 3 seed stitches of 3866 to create 1 seed head at the end of each of the 6 stems. C

FLOWERS & BUSH

Layering, layering, layering: stitching shrubbery and low growing plants is all about overlapping layers to create texture and dimension. The addition of flowers lends pops of color to a piece, which is fun to add and can help develop dimension.

TOOLS & MATERIALS

- 5″ (12.7cm) embroidery hoop
- Tapestry needle, size 26
- Chenille needle, size 26 (optional)
- Embroidery scissors
- Flowers & Bush Tutorial Pattern (page 156)
- Thimble (optional, but recommended)
- 7″ × 7″ (17.8 × 17.8cm) square of natural-colored cotton duck canvas
- DMC six-stranded cotton embroidery floss (colors below)

DMC THREAD COLORS

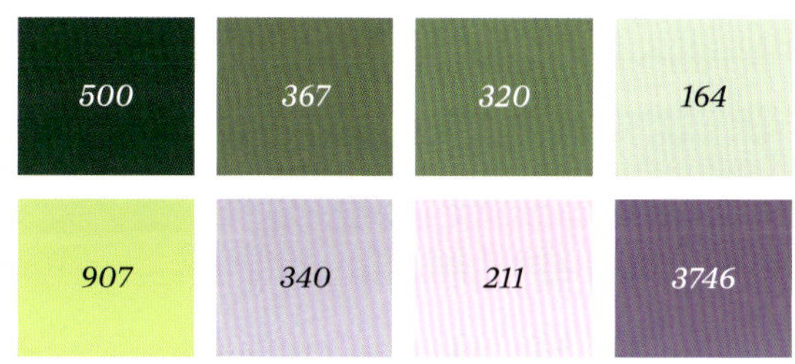

STITCHES USED

Satin Stitch, page 28

Seed Stitch, page 29

Long and Short Stitch, page 28

Straight Stitch, page 27

Split Back Stitch, page 28

Stab Stitch, page 29

COLOR GUIDE

TRANSFERRING THE PATTERN

Transfer the design onto the center of the 7″ × 7″ (17.8 × 17.8cm) fabric square (see Transferring Designs, page 17). Secure the fabric in the 5″ (12.7cm) hoop.

STITCHING

Use 2 strands of thread unless otherwise noted.

Bush: Right

1. Add satin stitches and seed stitches of 500 (all angled upward) to shade 9 small sections. A

Losing Guidelines Behind Stitches

When stitching this pattern, some of the guidelines for the flower stems will get lost as you work your way upward. Referring back to a photo of the pattern can help you remember where the stems should be placed.

2. Work upwards and blend 367 long and short stitches in between the 500 patches. Fan out straight stitches at the top of the section, as shown. B

3. Use long and short stitches in 320 to fill the remaining open space at the top. C

4. With 1 strand of 500, blend small seed stitches around the right side of the bush. Add them around the small open space at the bottom. D

5. Starting at the base, use 1 strand of 367 to add angled seed stitch leaves around the right side of the bush. Each cluster of leaves should have 3–4 stitches that share the same exit hole down through the top of the fabric. Overlap some of the 500 sections. E F

Stitching Through Thick Work

When the overlapping stitches start creating a thick layer of threads, it can be hard to push the needle through. Switching to a chenille needle with a sharper end might be helpful. Additionally, the use of a thimble may make pushing the needle through less demanding on the fingertips.

6. Repeat Step 5 with 1 strand of 320, creating more leaf clusters across the bush. G

7. Repeat Step 5 with 1 strand of 164 to create 6 leaf clusters across the center of the section. Then, add them to the top of the bush. H

8. Add seed stitches and leaf clusters with 1 strand of 907 above and across the top of the bush. I

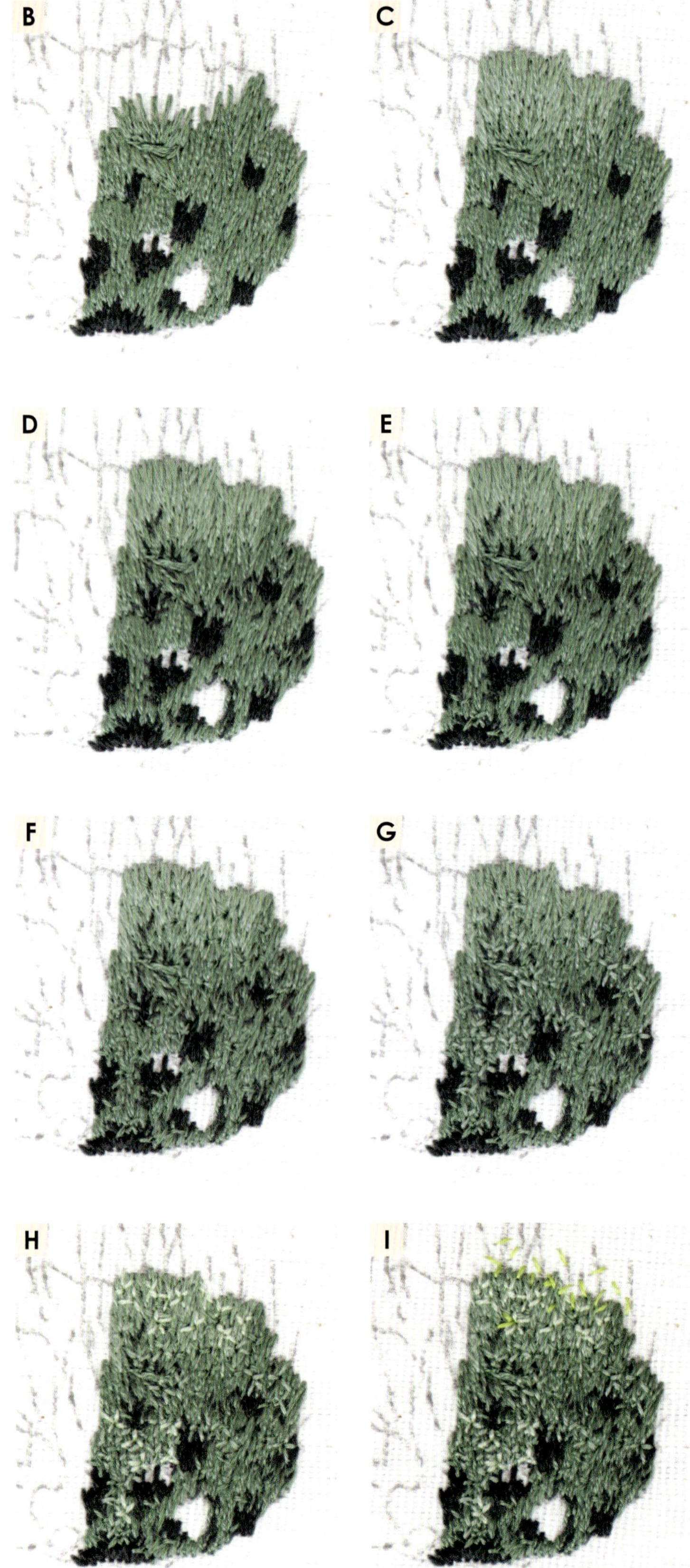

Bush: Left

1. Use long and short stitches of 500 to create 4 small patches. A

2. Fill in the bush with long and short stitches in 367, noting the direction of the stitches. B

3. Fill in the top 2 open spaces with long and short stitches of 320. C

4. Add small seed stitches with 1 strand of 500 across the left side of the bush, including near the open space. Blend them into the largest patch of 500. D

5. Repeat Step 5 in Bush: Right (left) with 1 strand of 367 to add leaf clusters across the left side of the bush. E

6. Repeat Step 5 with 1 strand of 320 to create more leaf clusters. F

7. Stitch more leaf clusters with 1 strand of 164, placing 3 near the open space at the bottom and 6 across the upper part of the bush. G

8. Add seed stitches and leaf clusters with 1 strand of 907 above and across the top of the bush. H

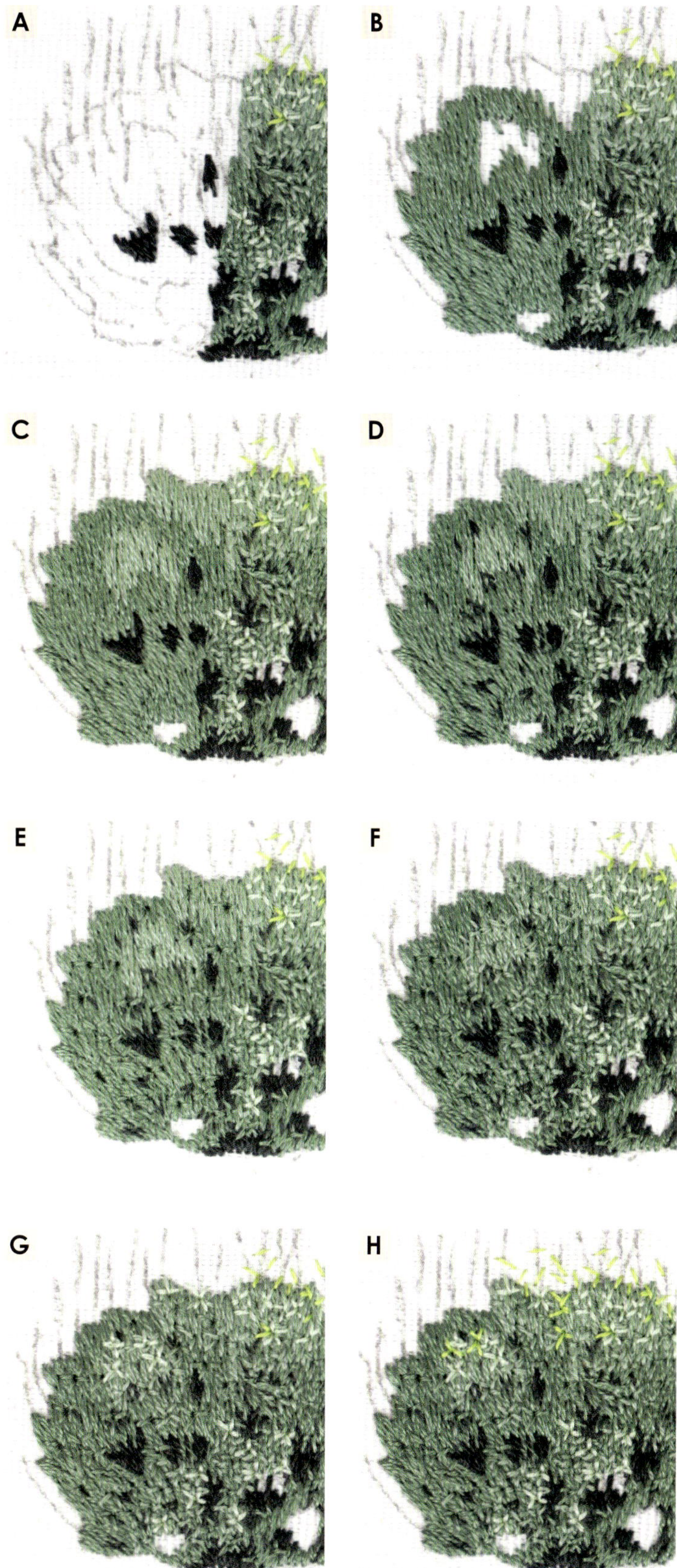

Flowers: Stems

1. Split back stitch with 1 strand of 500 to establish the stems. A B

Flowers: Blooms

1. Start at the bottom of the stem on the left. Use 340 to make seed stitches in a *V*-shape. Work your way up the stem, gradually making the stitches smaller as they near the top. Repeat to fill the first 3 stems. C

2. Skipping stems as shown, repeat Step 1 to fill 11 total stems. D

3. Blend small seed stitches into the flowers with 1 strand of 211. E

4. Blend small seed stitches into the lower halves of the flowers with 1 strand of 3746. F

5. Use 1 strand of 164 to add 1 stab stitch at the end of each flower stem. G

6. Repeat Step 1 to add seed stitch flowers in 340 to 7 more stems as shown. H

7. Repeat Steps 3–4 to add single strand seed stitches in 211 and 3746 to the flowers from Step 6. I

8. Repeat Step 1 to add seed stitch flowers in 340 to 3 more stems as shown, moving into the foreground. Repeat Steps 3–4 to add single strand seed stitches in 211 and 3746. J

A

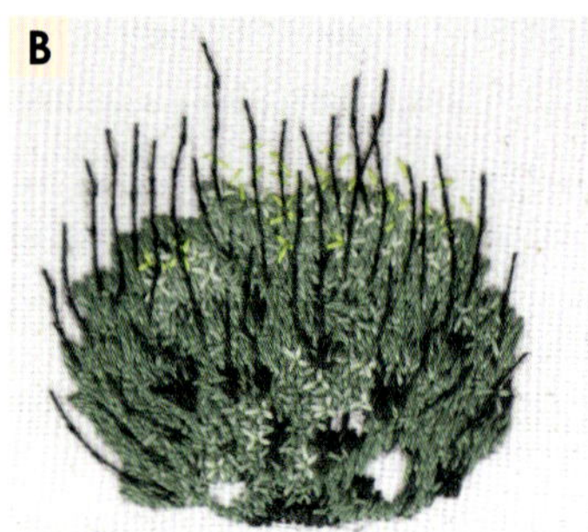
B

C

D

E

F

G

H

I

J

9. With 1 strand of 164, add stab stitches to the tops of the stems. K

10. Repeat Step 1 to add seed stitch flowers in 340 on 8 more stems in the foreground. L M

11. Use 1 strand of 211 to add angled seed stitches in between the 340 petals on the top halves of the first 3 stems (from the left). Repeat up the entire length of the next 2 stems. Repeat at the tops of the remaining Step 10 stems. N

12. With 1 strand of 3746, add small seed stitches to the lower halves of all the Step 10 flowers. O

13. Repeat Steps 10–12 on the remaining 3 bare stems. Use 211 on the top only of the first and third flowers. Use 211 across the entire second flower. Add 3746 to the bottom of all flowers. P

14. With 1 strand of 164, add stab stitches to the tops of the stems. Q

15. Use angled and overlapping 340 seed stitches to fill in the remaining open spaces near the bottom of the bush. R

16. Highlight the Step 15 patches with angled and overlapping seed stitches of 1 strand of 211. Repeat with 1 strand of 3746. S

17. With 1 strand of 164, add stab stitches to the ends of the 211 highlights from Step 16. T

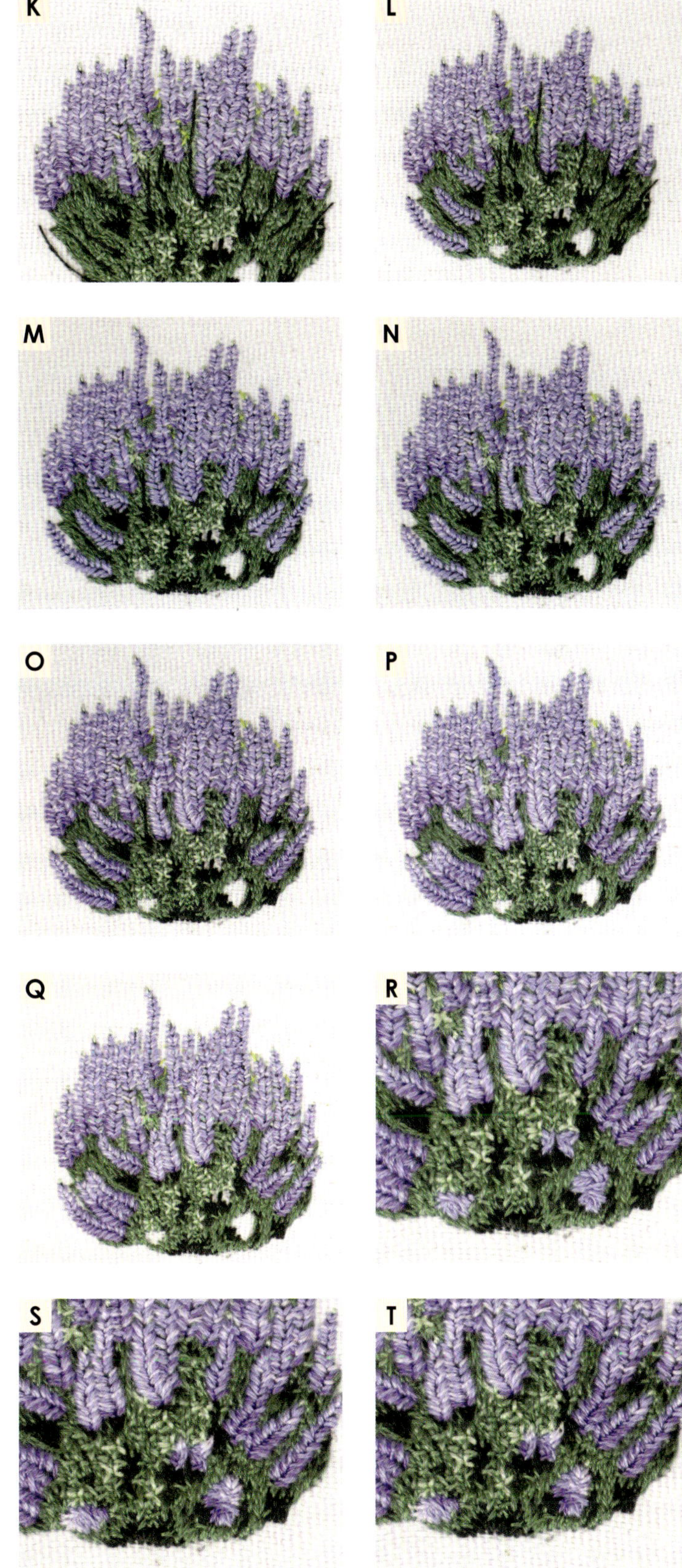

CALM WATER

Stitching a magnified version of calm water can help you see, and better understand, the many different colors and directional changes sometimes required to create the movement of this element.

TOOLS & MATERIALS

- 5″ (12.7cm) embroidery hoop
- Tapestry needle, size 26
- Embroidery scissors
- Calm Water Tutorial Pattern (page 156)
- 7″ × 7″ (17.8 × 17.8cm) square of natural-colored cotton duck canvas
- DMC six-stranded cotton embroidery floss (colors below)

DMC THREAD COLORS

STITCHES USED

Long and Short Stitch, page 28

Seed Stitch, page 29

Split Back Stitch, page 28

Straight Stitch, page 27

COLOR GUIDE

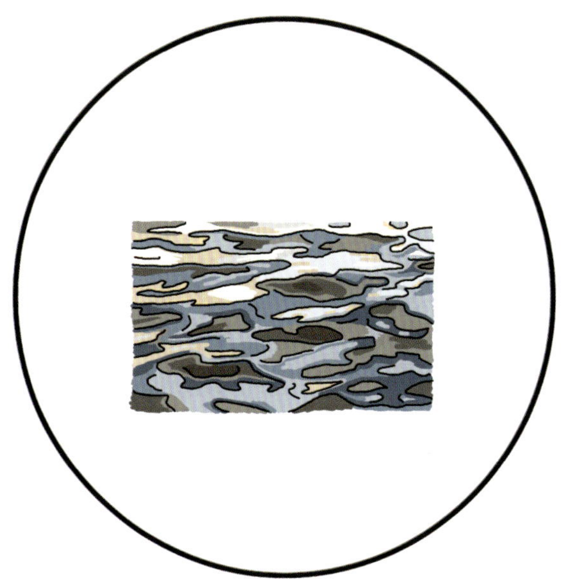

TRANSFERRING THE PATTERN

Transfer the design onto the center of the 7″ × 7″ (17.8 × 17.8cm) fabric square (see Transferring Designs, page 17). Secure the fabric in the 5″ (12.7cm) hoop.

STITCHING

Use 2 strands of thread unless otherwise noted.

Bottom Right

1. Long and short stitch one patch of 3799 near the center of the water. Then, add long and short stitches and seed stitches of 413, blending one section into the 3799 patch. A

Creating Movement

The angles of the stitches create the movement of the water. Slanting the stitches to match the angles of the guidelines is important in representing the fluidity of this element (see Creating Movement, page 20).

A

2. With long and short stitches and seed stitches, blend in sections of 169. B

3. Use 930 long and short stitches and seed stitches to shade around the 169 stitches, as shown. Leave open spaces as indicated by the Color Guide. C

4. Blend in 931 split back stitches to line borders. Use long and short stitches and seed stitches to fill in the larger spaces. D

5. Fill and blend with long and short stitches of 932. Use seed stitches at the left edge, upper right, and lower right of the stitched area. E

6. Fill the remaining open space with long and short stitches of 613. F

7. With 1 strand of 932, split back stitch a line of highlights. Add overlapping seed stitches to connect the 169 patches to the right. G

Bottom Left

1. Long and short stitch one patch with 3799. Blend in long and short stitches of 413. Add more patches of 413. A

2. Blend in 169 with long and short stitches. Stitch around the existing patches with split back stitches. Add a couple patches with seed stitches. B

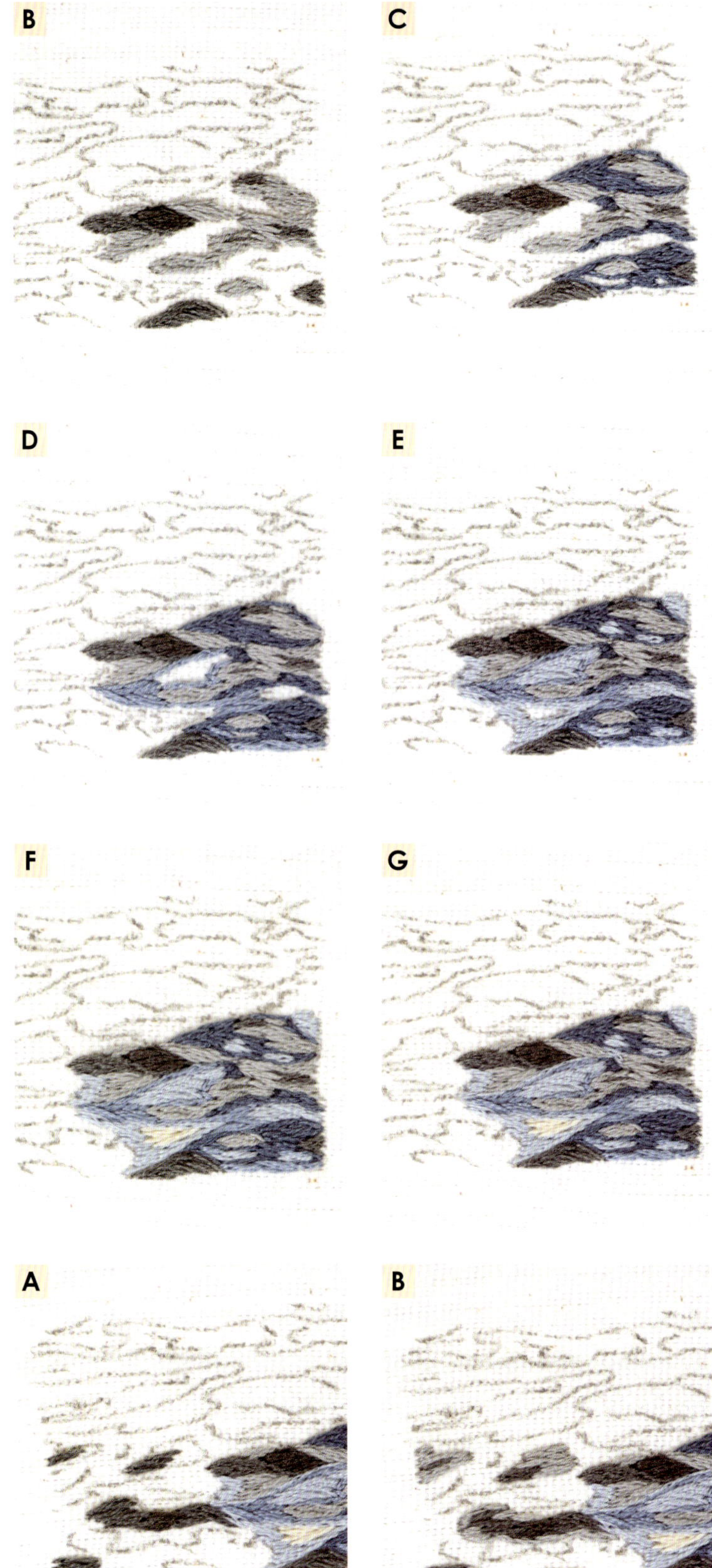

3. Split back stitch the lines with 930, then fill in the rest of the 930 shapes with seed stitches and split back stitches. C

4. Blend in 931 long and short stitches, connecting the shapes. Use seed stitches and straight stitches for the lower area. D

5. Blend in 2–3 seed stitches of 932 at the top border of the stitches from Step 4, then continue blending in with long and short stitches. E

6. Use long and short stitches of 932 to fill in the open space across the bottom. Shade the open space with split back stitches. Fill the rest of the space with long and short stitches of 613. F G

7. Use 1 strand of 169 to edge straight stitches between the 2 patches of 613. Use 1 strand of 932 to split back stitch above the patch of 613 and above the 930 stitches on the right side. Use 1 strand of 168 to blend straight stitches into the 613 patches. H

Top Left

1. Fill in sections with long and short stitches, straight stitches, and seed stitches of 413 and 169. A

2. Fill in patches of 931 with long and short stitches. B

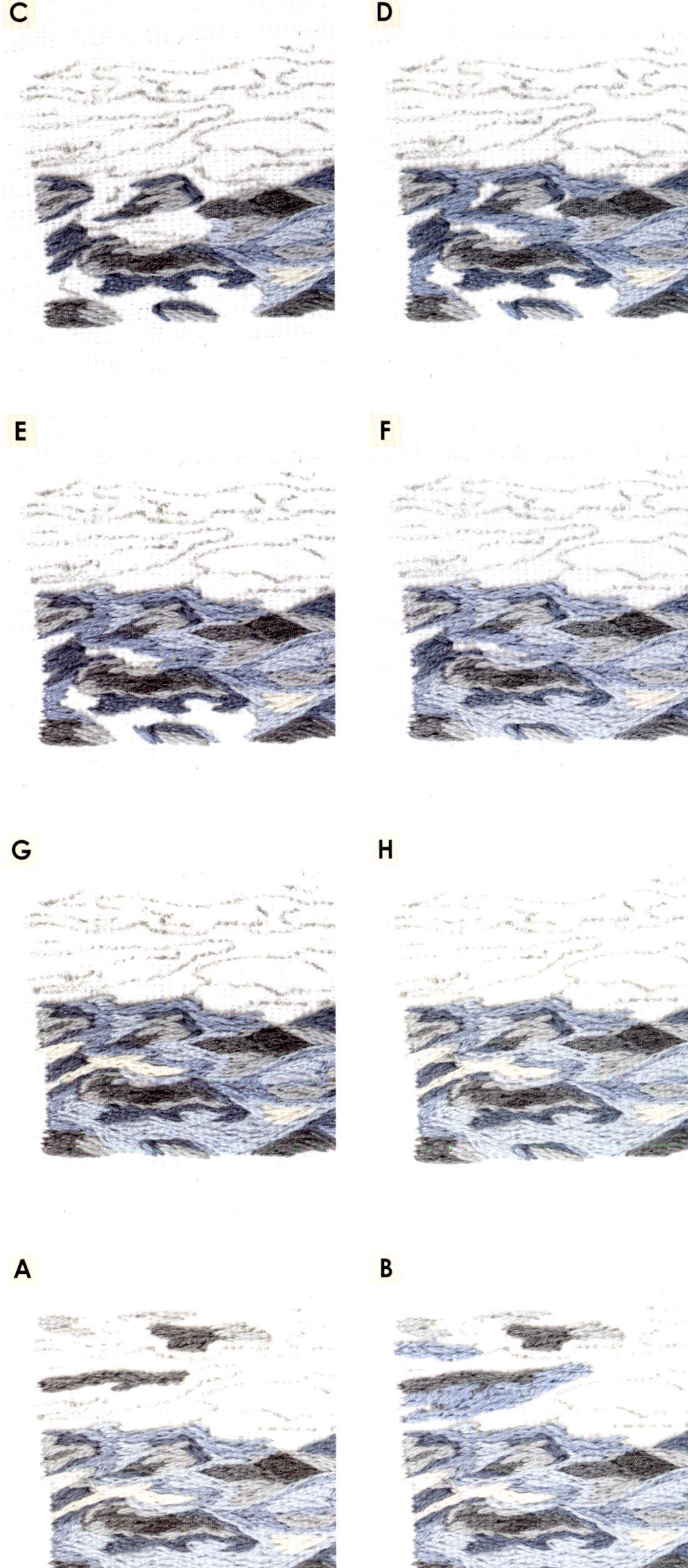

3. Blend in 932 long and short stitches and straight stitches. C

4. Blend in 613 long and short stitches and seed stitches. Add a section of overlapping split back stitches along the top. D

5. Blend in long and short stitches of 168 at the top border, then fill below with the same color. E

6. Fill the remaining open space at the top border with long and short stitches of 712, then use 1 strand to blend straight stitches into the 168 patches. F

7. Use 1 strand of 3865 to blend long and short stitches into the 712 stitches in the upper left corner. Use 1 strand of 931 to add split back stitches along the top of both 413 patches. Add several 738 accent seed stitches to the edges of the 613 patches. G

Adding Warmth

The subtle addition of warmer colors layered with the cool tones enhances the realism of the water, making it look like light is bouncing off the water's surface.

Top Right

1. Add several overlapping seed stitches of 3799 near the center. Blend in 413 seed stitches and straight stitches. Add new sections of 413. A B

2. Blend in long and short stitches and seed stitches of 169. C

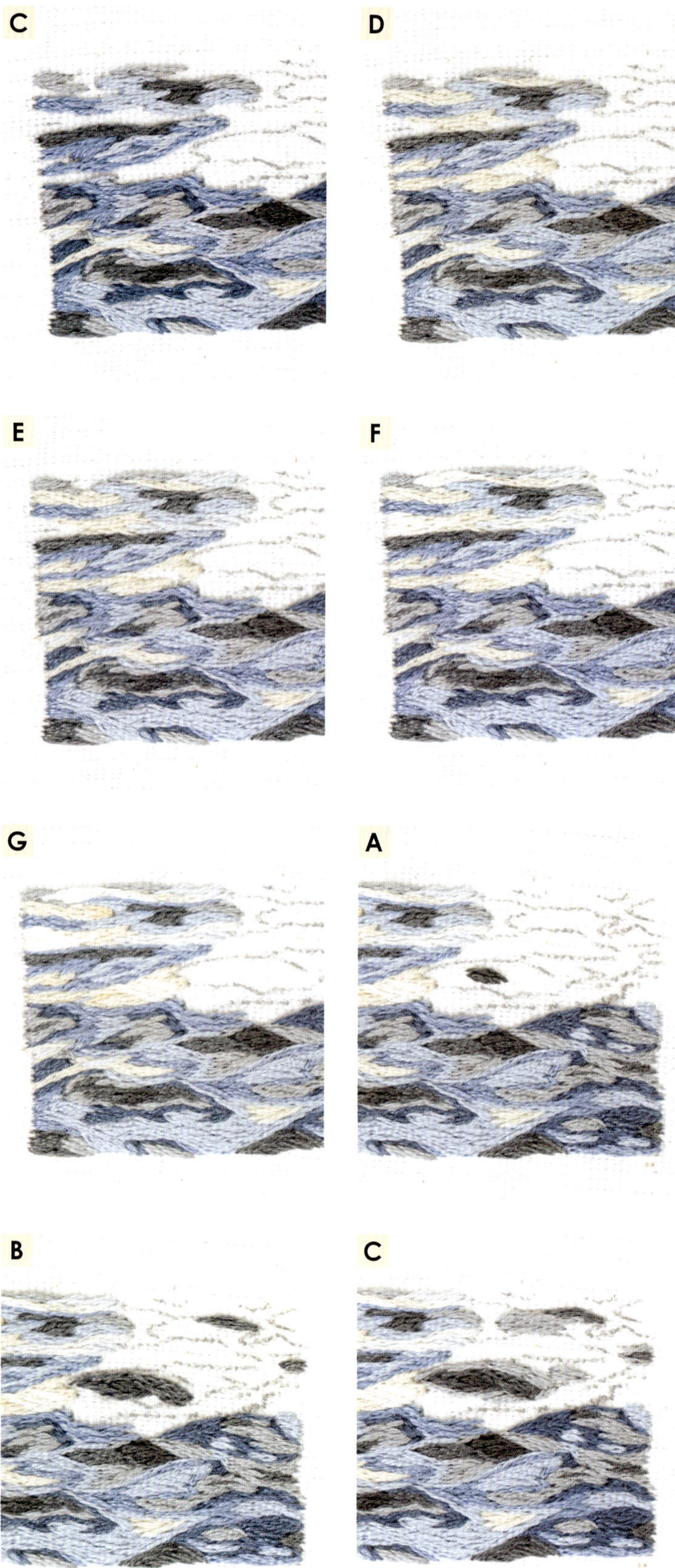

3. Blend in long and short stitches and seed stitches of 931. D

4. Fill in long and short stitches in 931, connecting the stitched areas. Add several overlapping seed stitches at the right border. E

5. Add 3 small patches of 932 seed stitches at the top border. Blend in long and short stitches and seed stitches below, following the curves. F

6. Fill the open space at the top with long and short stitches of 712. Add 1 seed stitch and straight stitch at the right border. G

7. Fill the remaining open space with 3753 long and short stitches. H

8. Blend overlapping seed stitches around the 169 stitches with 1 strand of 930. I

9. Blend straight and seed stitches of 613 into the 3753 patches. Use 1 strand of 3865 to blend overlapping straight stitches into the large 3753 patch. Use 1 strand of 738 to blend accent seed stitches into the lighter patches. J

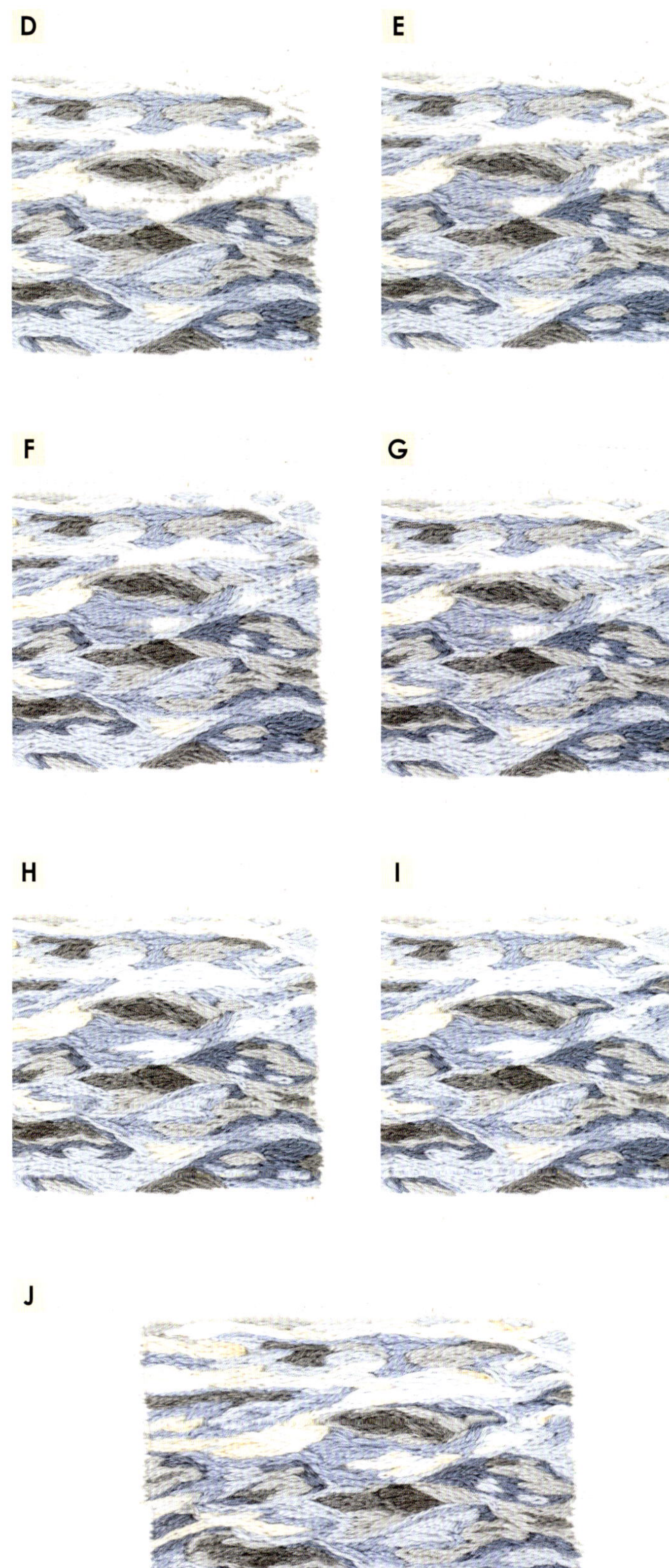

WAVE

Fluid stitching is essential for embroidering waves (see Creating Movement, page 20). After the structure of the wave is completed, go back and layer subtle accent stitches for the whitewater.

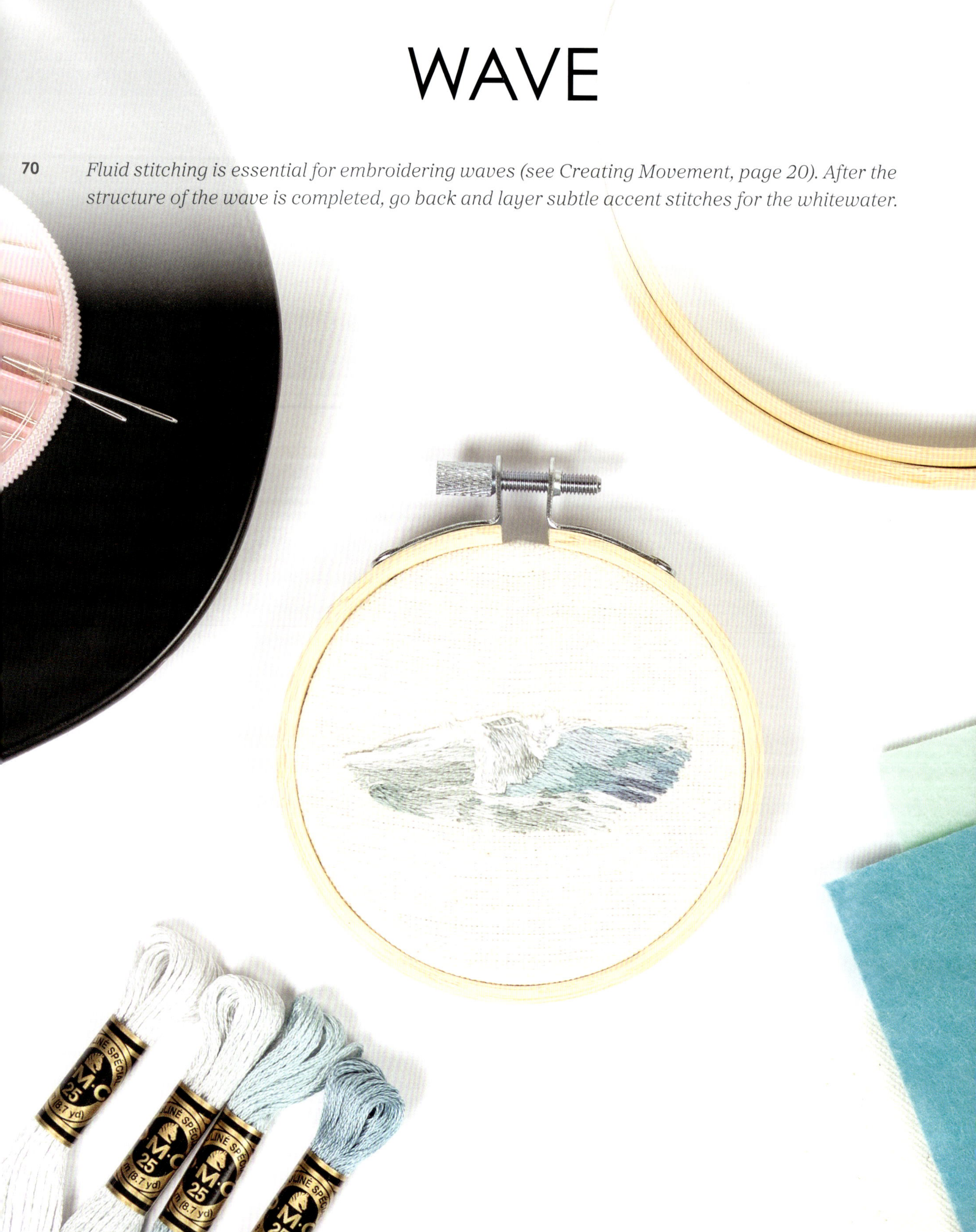

TOOLS & MATERIALS

- 5″ (12.7cm) embroidery hoop
- Tapestry needle, size 26
- Embroidery scissors
- Wave Tutorial Pattern (page 156)
- 7″ × 7″ (17.8 × 17.8cm) square of natural-colored cotton duck canvas
- DMC six-stranded cotton embroidery floss (colors below)

DMC THREAD COLORS

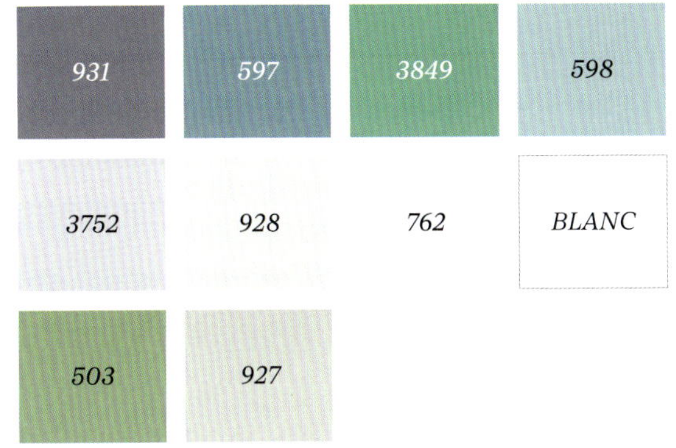

STITCHES USED

Long and Short Stitch, page 28

Straight Stitch, page 27

Seed Stitch, page 29

Stab Stitch, page 29

Split Back Stitch, page 28

Satin Stitch, page 28

COLOR GUIDE

TRANSFERRING THE PATTERN

Transfer the design onto the center of the 7″ × 7″ (17.8 × 17.8cm) fabric square (see Transferring Designs, page 17). Secure the fabric in the 5″ (12.7cm) hoop.

STITCHING

Use 2 strands of thread unless otherwise noted.

Right

1. Blend long and short stitches of 931 and 597 in the bottom right. **A**

2. Blend in long and short stitches of 3849, building a gradient. Leave an open patch for the next color. Blend in long and short stitches of 598. **B**

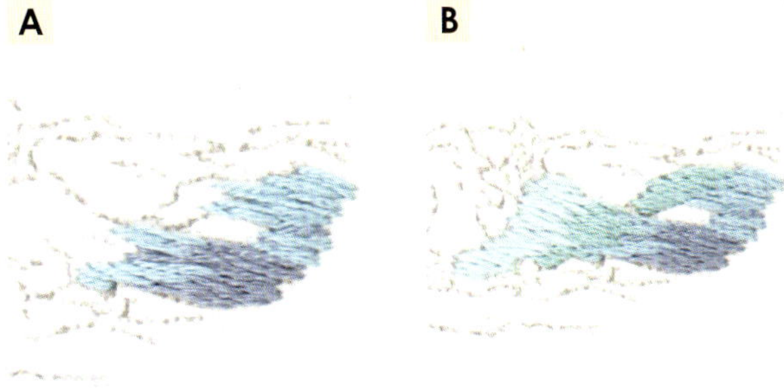

3. Fill the open patch and shade the upper section with long and short stitches of 3752. Blend straight and seed stitches below. C

4. Blend in more long and short stitches of 598 at the top. Add a couple seed stitches to blend. D

5. Add long and short stitches of 928 to shade the top right corner. Use 1 strand to blend angled seed stitches and stab stitches into the section below. Use 762 long and short stitches to fill the remaining spaces along the top border. Blend in 1 seed stitch below with 1 strand. E F

6. Blend seed stitches along the top border and right border with 1 strand of BLANC. Add seed stitches into the 928 patch with 1 strand of 597. G

Accent Stitches

Layering stab stitches and seed stitches produces the appearance of bubbles on the water's surface, while the light colors create the foam and reflections.

Left

1. Build up long and short stitches of 503. Use seed stitches as needed to create the shapes. A

2. Blend in long and short stitches of 927, filling in space along the left and bottom of the wave. B

3. Blend in long and short stitches of 928. Use split back stitches and seed stitches along the borders of existing shapes as needed. C

4. Use a combination of 503 seed stitches and satin stitches to add shapes to the right bottom side. Then, blend in 762 long and short stitches to fill the space. D E

5. With 1 strand of BLANC, edge the top of the 762 stitches from Step 4 with straight stitches. Blend in stab stitches.

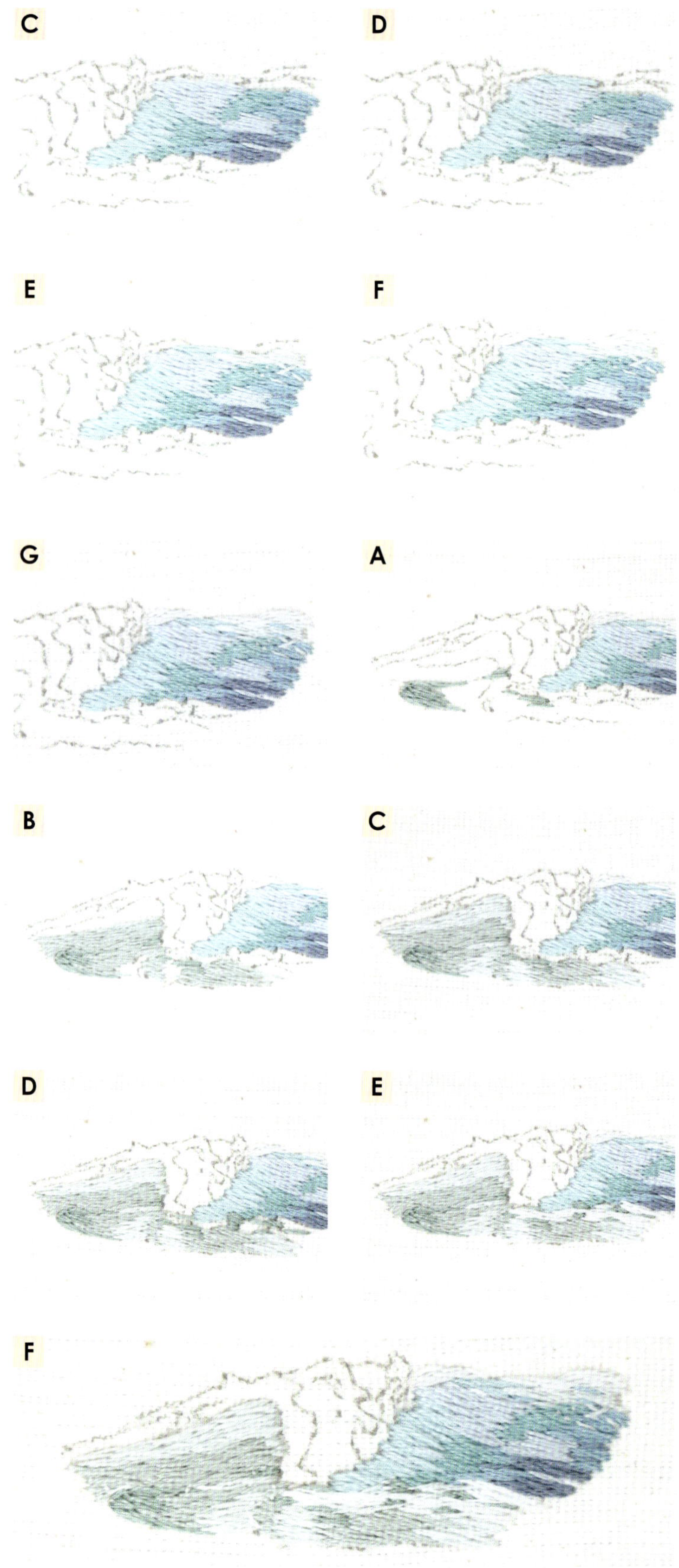

Create curved seed stitches around the left side. Use 1 strand of 928 to add seed stitches to the 762 stitches, tilting them opposite existing stitches. F

Top

1. Fill in long and short stitches of 927 at the crest and top left corner. A

The Lip

Creating the impression of a smooth breaking wave is all about placing stitches at uniform angles. Try working across the top of the lip at the same moderate slant, then gradually increasing the tilt with each row of added stitches.

2. Blend in long and short stitches of 928. B

3. Blend in more long and short stitches of 927. Add seed stitches of 3752 to blend the 927 and 928 sections. C

4. Use BLANC long and short stitches across the top left corner. Fill the top portion of the wave crest with angled BLANC seed stitches. Curve overlapping BLANC straight stitches down the open space. D

5. Seed stitch with 928 over the top left BLANC stitches. Fill the open space between the BLANC stitches with seed stitches of 762. Add satin stitches of the same color to the center open space. E

6. Edge BLANC split back stitches along the top of the crest. Then, with a combination of satin stitches and angled seed stitches of the same color, fill the remaining open space to the right. F

7. Use 1 strand of 3752 to add seed stitches to the 762 satin stitches. Use 1 strand of BLANC to straight stitch across the central 927 stitches from Step 1, then blend in a couple seed stitches. Add several stab stitches above the wave to represent seaspray. G

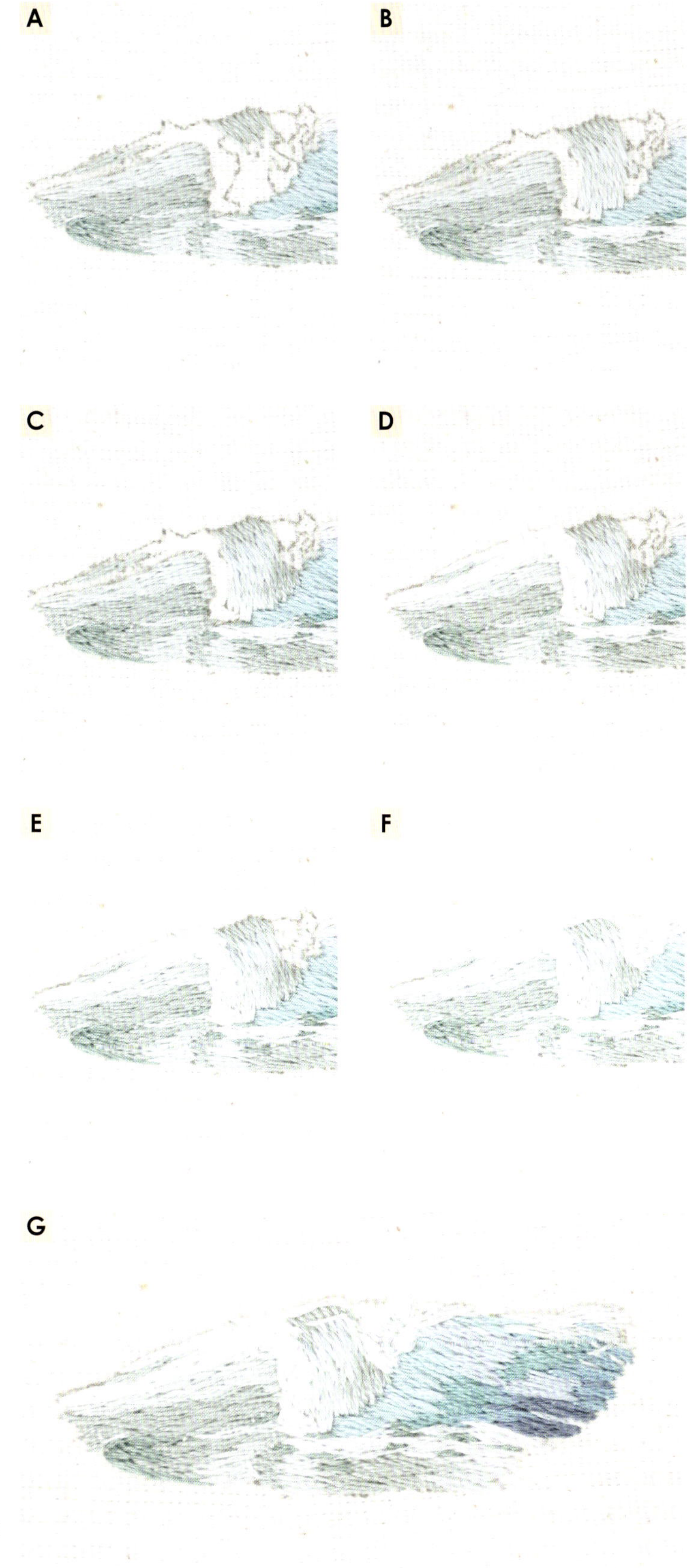

SAND

Thread painting sand can be a test in color perception, especially when working from a reference photo. Often, the value change is so subtle that it's hard to tell when and where a color shift actually takes place. The more colors you have on hand, the smoother the gradient will be (see Blending & Mixing Colors, page 20).

TOOLS & MATERIALS

- 5″ (12.7cm) embroidery hoop
- Tapestry needle, size 26
- Embroidery scissors
- Sand Tutorial Pattern (page 157)
- 7″ × 7″ (17.8 × 17.8cm) square of natural-colored cotton duck canvas
- DMC six-stranded cotton embroidery floss (colors below)

DMC THREAD COLORS

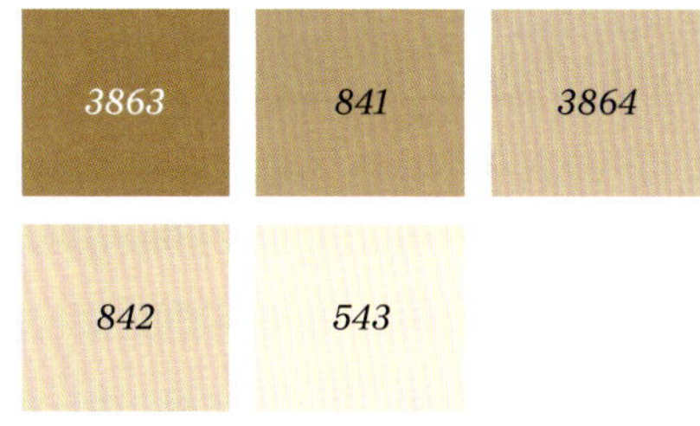

STITCHES USED

Long and Short Stitch, page 28

Split Back Stitch, page 28

Satin Stitch, page 28

Straight Stitch, page 27

Seed Stitch, page 29

COLOR GUIDE

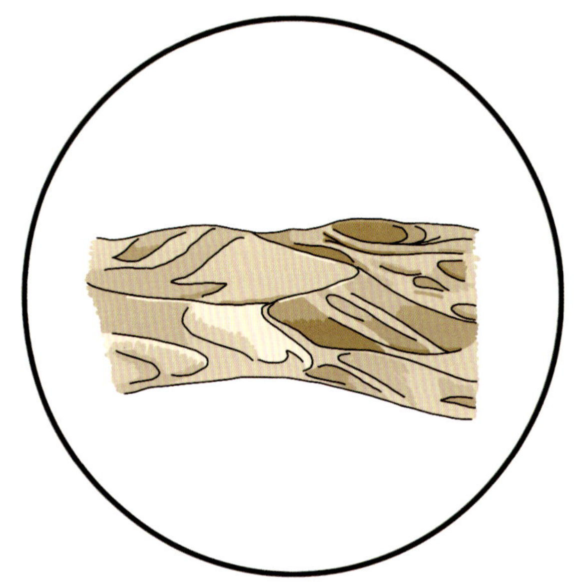

STITCH FLOW GUIDE

TRANSFERRING THE PATTERN

Transfer the design onto the center of the 7″ × 7″ (17.8 × 17.8cm) fabric square (see Transferring Designs, page 17). Secure the fabric in the 5″ (12.7cm) hoop.

STITCHING

Use 2 strands of thread unless otherwise noted.

Background Sand

1. Begin to fill in long and short stitches of 3863. Use split back stitches for the lines. A

Start With Dark

Being able to differentiate the midtones from the highlights and shadows can take practice, but I find it's easiest to start with the darkest shades, then work my way to the lighter ones.

2. Blend in long and short stitches of 841. Split back stitch the lines. Use satin and straight stitches at the right border. B

3. Blend in long and short stitches of 3864. C

4. Blend in 842 split back stitches and long and short stitches, filling the rest of the open space and following the Stitch Flow Guide. Use 1 strand of 842 to edge the darkest depressions. D

Right Slopes

1. Shade the slope with long and short stitches of 3863. Use split back stitches and seed stitches for the smaller areas. E

2. Blend in long and short stitches and seed stitches of 841. F

3. Build up the gradient by blending in long and short stitches of 3864. Stitch small perpendicular straight stitches in the bottom right corner. G

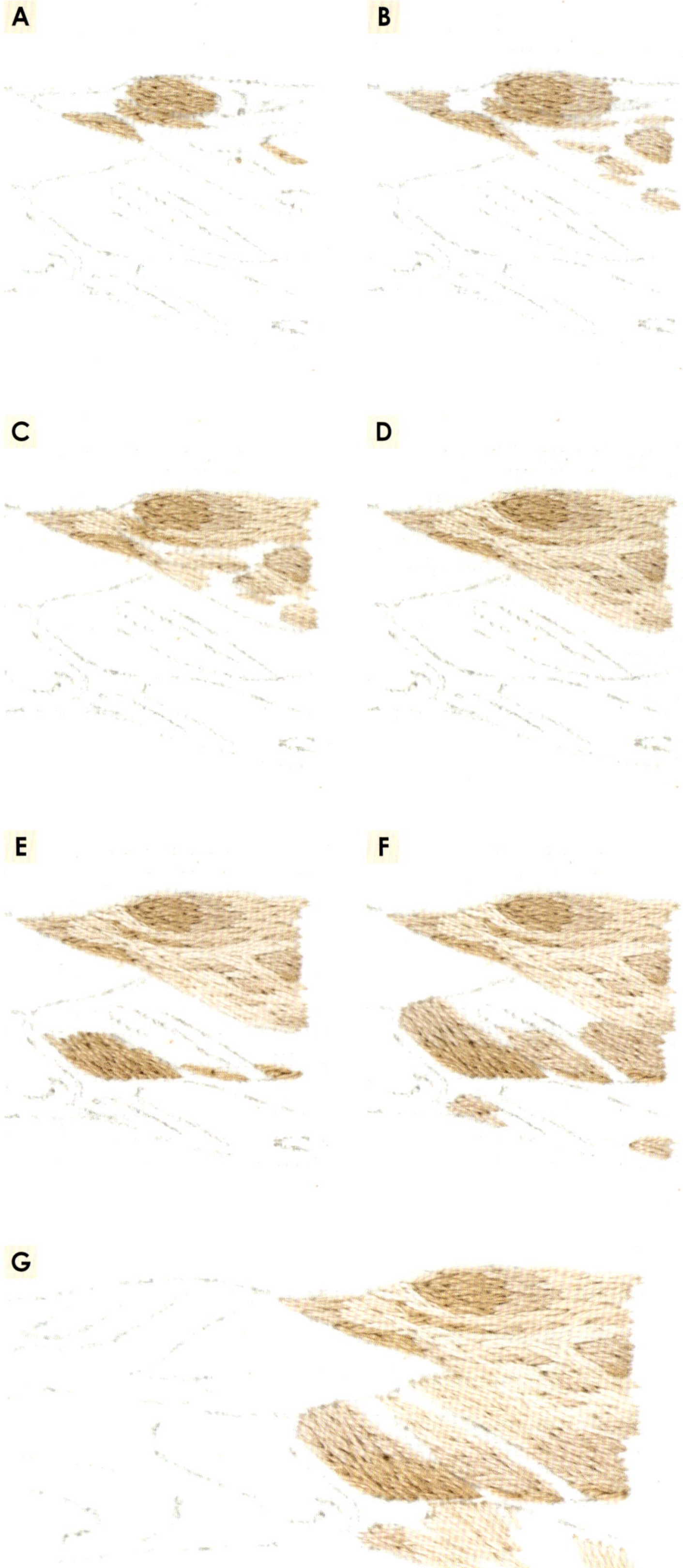

4. Blend in long and short stitches and split backstitches of 842. Fill the remaining open space. H I

Top Left Slope

1. Use long and short stitches in 841 to shade. Use split back stitches for the lines. A

2. Blend in long and short stitches of 3864. B

3. Fill the remaining space on the slope with long and short stitches of 842. Split back stitch along the curved ridge with 1 strand. Seed stitch at the curved point of the slope. With 1 strand of 543, add 3 straight stitches to highlight the crests of the slopes. C

Bottom Left Slope

1. Fill in the upper section with long and short stitches of 3864. Shade the lower left with seed stitches and split back stitches. D

2. Blend in long and short stitches and seed stitches of 842, referring to the Stitch Flow Guide. E

3. Fill the remaining open space with long and short stitches of 543. With 1 strand of the same color, line the ridges with split back stitches. F

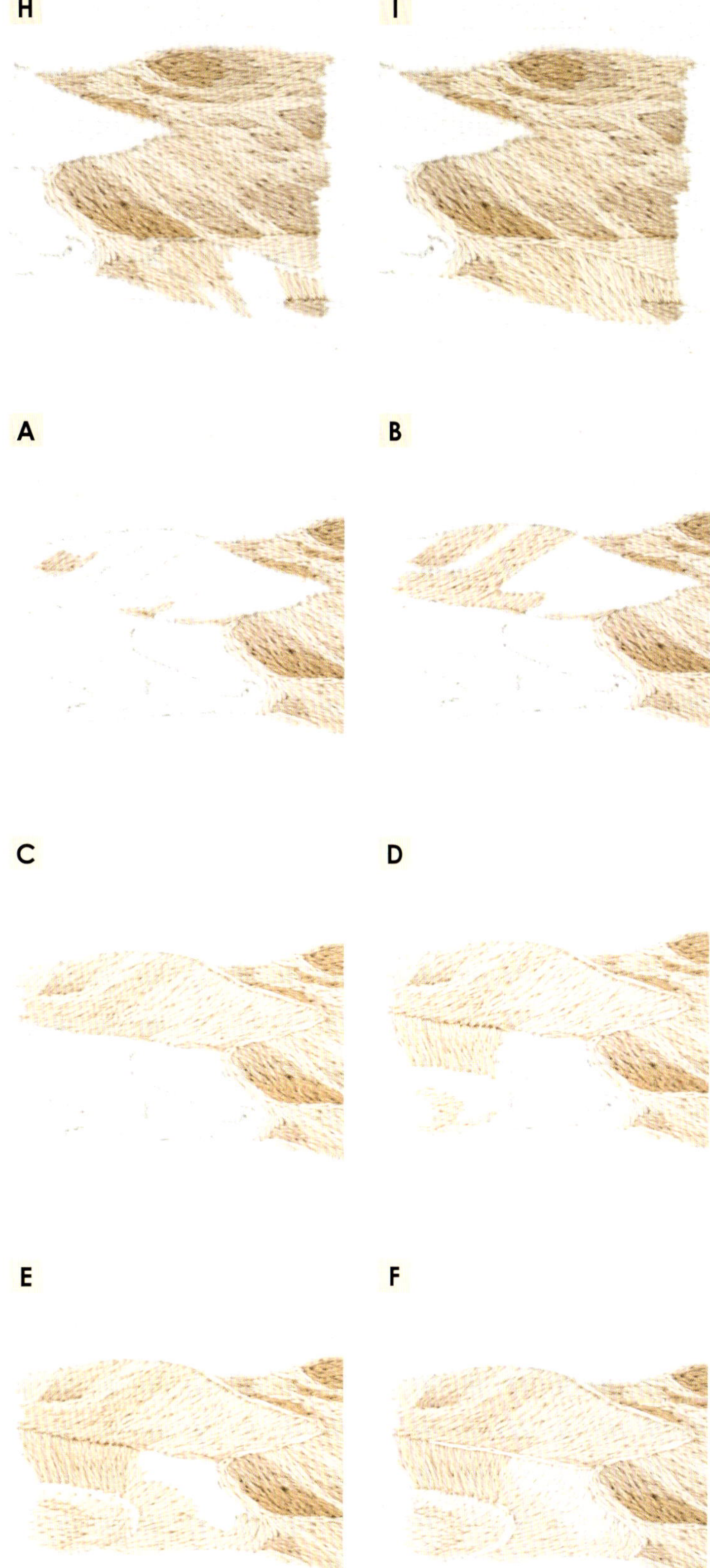

ROCK

Strategically placing rocks in a landscape thread painting produces nice focal points that can lead the viewer's eye through the scene. The addition of this element can also balance a scene—the hard, solid, and sometimes jagged surfaces of rocks pair well with the smooth fluidity of water, or a flowing meadow of tall grasses (see Deciding Which Elements To Incorporate, page 14).

TOOLS & MATERIALS

- 5″ (12.7cm) embroidery hoop
- Tapestry needle, size 26
- Embroidery scissors
- Rock Tutorial Pattern (page 157)
- 7″ × 7″ (17.8 × 17.8cm) square of natural-colored cotton duck canvas
- DMC six-stranded cotton embroidery floss (colors below)

DMC THREAD COLORS

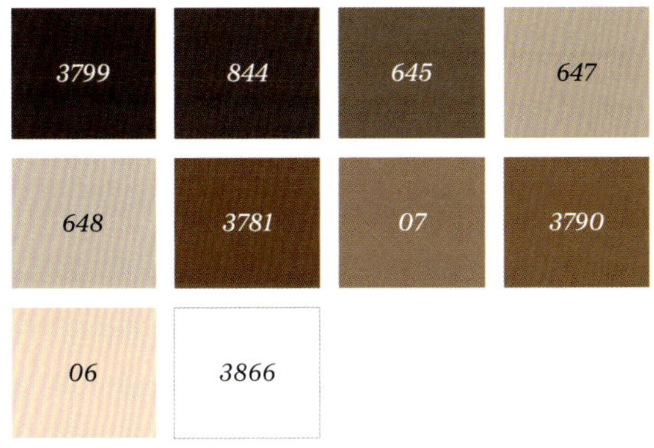

STITCHES USED

Long and Short Stitch, page 28

Satin Stitch, page 28

Split Back Stitch, page 28

Seed Stitch, page 29

Straight Stitch, page 27

Stab Stitch, page 29

COLOR GUIDE

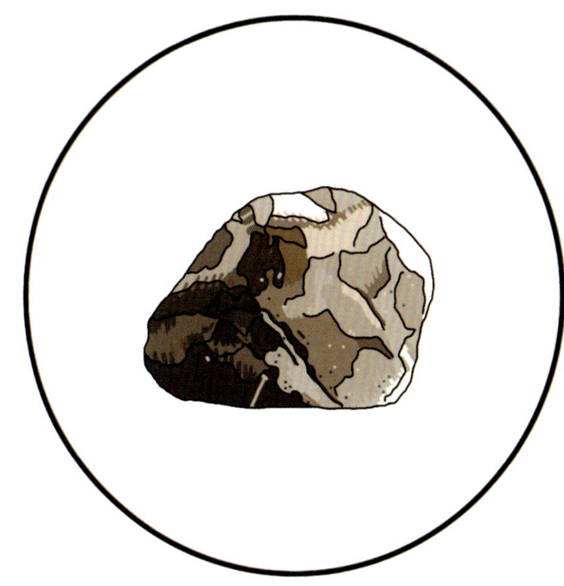

TRANSFERRING THE PATTERN

Transfer the design onto the center of the 7″ × 7″ (17.8 × 17.8cm) fabric square (see Transferring Designs, page 17). Secure the fabric in the 5″ (12.7cm) hoop.

STITCHING

Use 2 strands of thread unless otherwise noted.

Left

1. Fill in sections of 3799 at the bottom with long and short stitches and satin stitches. Add split back stitches for the lines and seed stitches for the angled fans of stitching. Use 1 strand to connect the upper right patches with seed stitches. **A**

A

2. Shade in 844 satin stitches and long and short stitches along and above the sweeping border. Blend in seed stitches and satin stitches with the existing 3799 stitches below the border. **B**

3. Use long and short stitches and seed stitches of 645 to fill the bottom left section. Seed stitch and long and short stitch the areas higher on the rock. **C**

4. Blend in long and short stitches of 647 across the rock. Add 1 straight stitch above the lower border. Then, fill the remaining space with long and short stitches of 648. Switch to 1 strand of 648, and seed stitch and stab stitch to accent the darker colors. **D**

Laying the Base Color Before the Details

When working on a section that has smaller details, like the dark spots on the rock face, it is easiest to lay down the color that makes up the majority of the area first, then blend or stitch the smaller details or color changes on top of those.

5. Add seed stitches of 3781 throughout the section. Blend straight stitches of 07 into 648 at the bottom border. Stab stitch with 1 strand of 3799 across the lower right section. **E**

Right

1. Fill in sections of long and short stitches of 3790 and 07. Use seed stitches to blend between the colors. Use seed stitches of 07 to create an angled line of stitches to the upper right. **A**

2. Blend in long and short stitches, seed stitches, and satin stitches of 647 across the right side of the rock. **B**

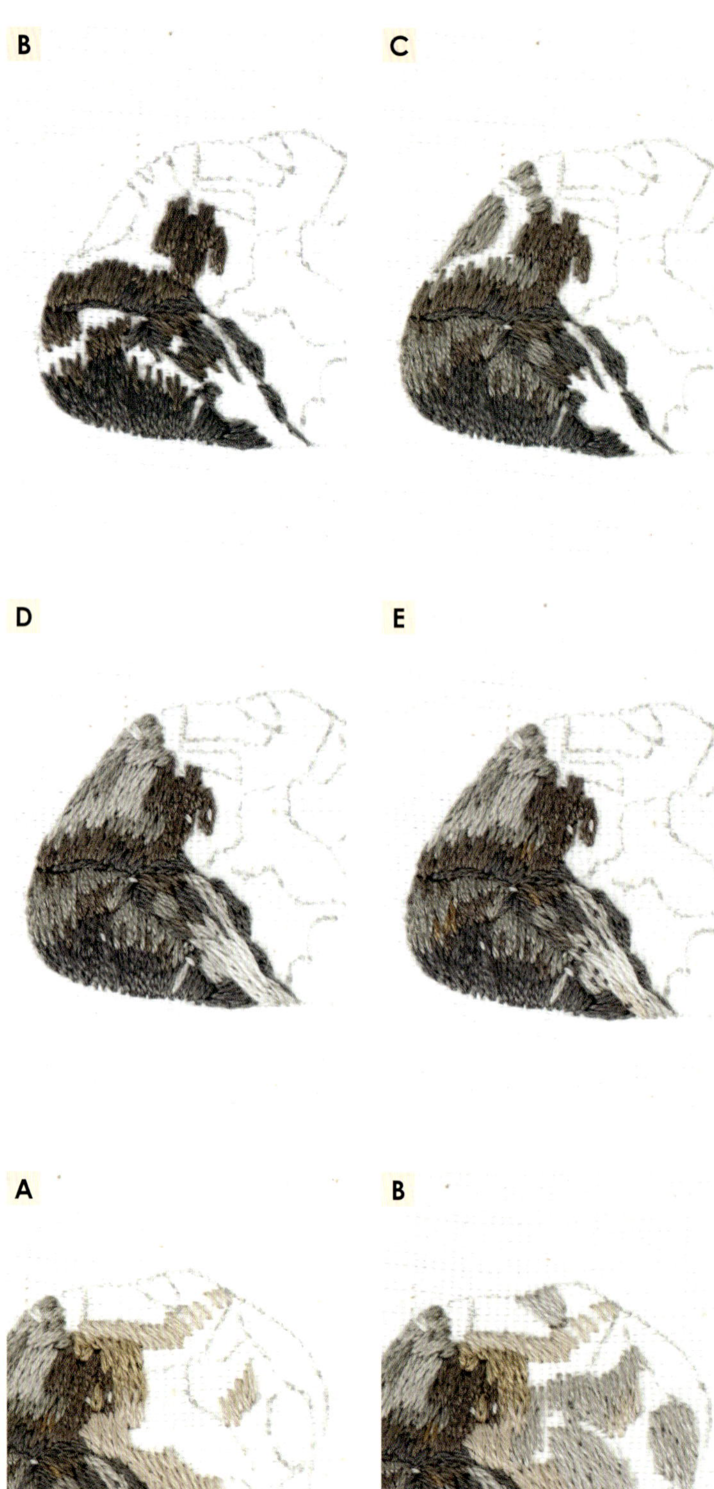

3. Blend in long and short stitches and satin stitches of 648 to continue filling the rock. C

4. Fill in the central open spaces with long and short stitches of 06. D

5. Fill the open spaces along the borders with long and short stitches of 3866. Fan out overlapping 645 seed stitches to fill in the remaining open space. E

6. Blend the gradient between 3866 and 07 at the top of the rock with 1 strand of 06 seed stitches between the 2 colors. Use 1 strand of 06 to seed and stab stitch across the darker areas of the rock. F

7. Use 1 strand of 3799 to seed and stab stitch to the right of the existing 3799 sections across the whole rock. Use 1 strand of 645 to stab stitch in the lower right corner. Then split back stitch above the 06 stitches in the center. G

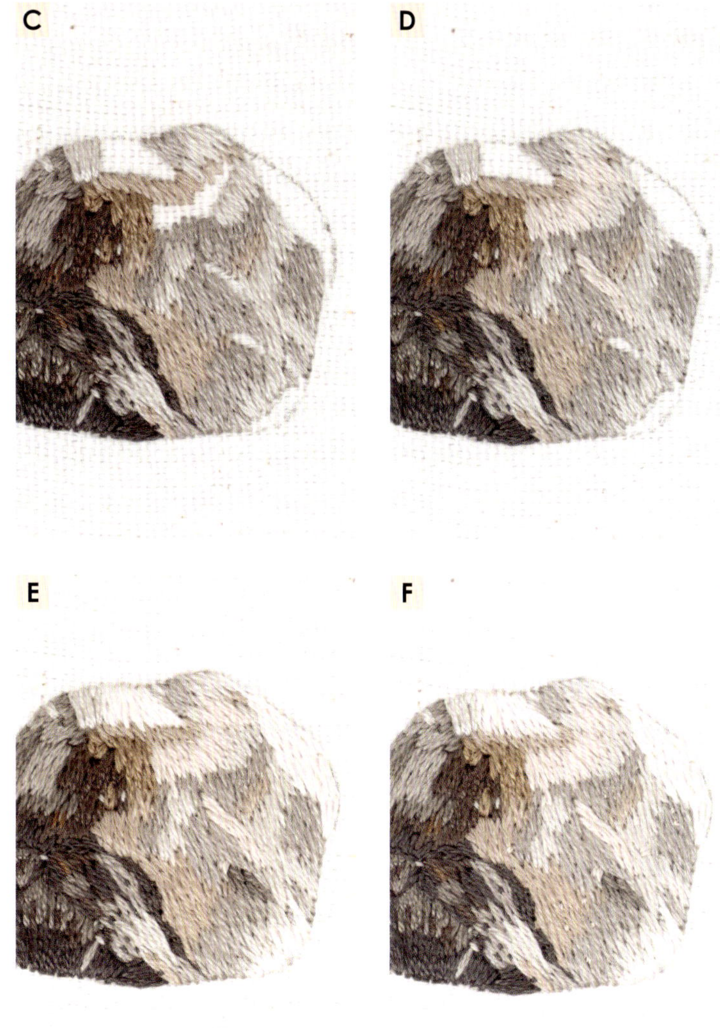

Landscape PROJECTS

Because there are so many details in each landscape project, each one comes with a Color Guide. The color guides give you a visual breakdown of where each color is placed, which can be helpful in comparison to the blended colors in the step-by-step images. Remember to refer to the list of DMC threads for the exact colors used. Reference the Stitch Library (page 26) for instructions on any unfamiliar stitches. All projects are finished in a 3″ (7.6cm) display hoop.

ROLLING HILLSIDE

When I first started thread painting, I mostly created scenes with multiple hills because it was an approachable way to create depth and practice stitch direction changes. Adding pops of color with small flower details makes this type of landscape really enjoyable. Inspired by the hills near Gaviota, CA during the last superbloom, this project incorporates sky, cloud, hill, and flower landscape elements (see Landscape Element Tutorials, page 30).

TOOLS & MATERIALS

- 5″ (12.7cm) embroidery hoop
- 3″ (7.6cm) beech display hoop (optional)
- Tapestry needle, size 26
- Embroidery scissors
- Rolling Hillside Pattern (page 157)
- Hoop stand (optional)
- 7″ × 7″ (17.8 × 17.8cm) square of natural-colored cotton duck canvas
- DMC six-stranded cotton embroidery floss (colors below)

COLOR GUIDE

TRANSFERRING THE PATTERN

Transfer the design onto the center of the 7″ × 7″ (17.8 × 17.8cm) fabric square (see Transferring Designs, page 17). Secure the fabric in the 5″ (12.7cm) working hoop.

STITCHING

Use 2 strands of thread unless otherwise noted.

DMC THREAD COLORS

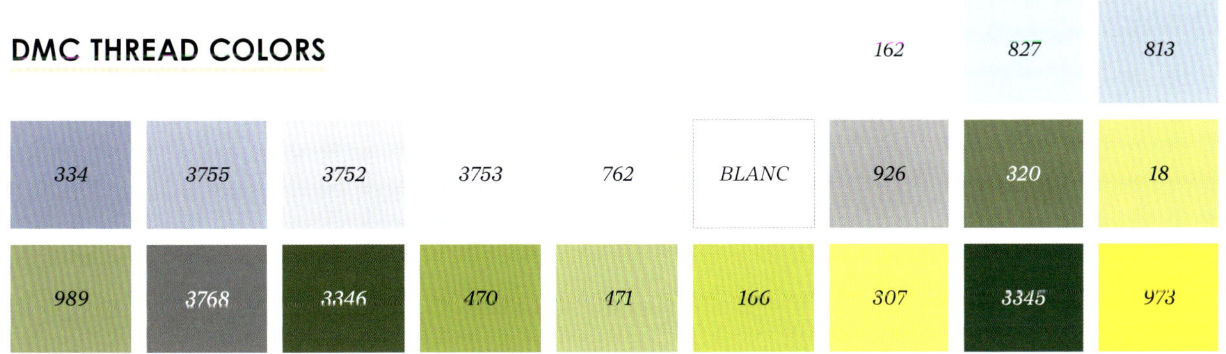

Sky

1. Blend and fill the sky, starting at the bottom, using horizontal long and short stitches of 162 and 827. Use straight stitches to blend the 2 colors. Work around the clouds and against the hills using seed stitches as needed. **A**

2. Blend in 813 long and short stitches and straight stitches to fill the rest of the sky. **B**

Clouds

1. Begin filling the large cloud. Use long and short stitches and seed stitches. Start with 334, blending with the sky. Then, blend in patches of 3755. Finally, introduce 3752 seed stitches and long and short stitches to sweep through the center of the cloud and connect the existing stitches. **C** **D**

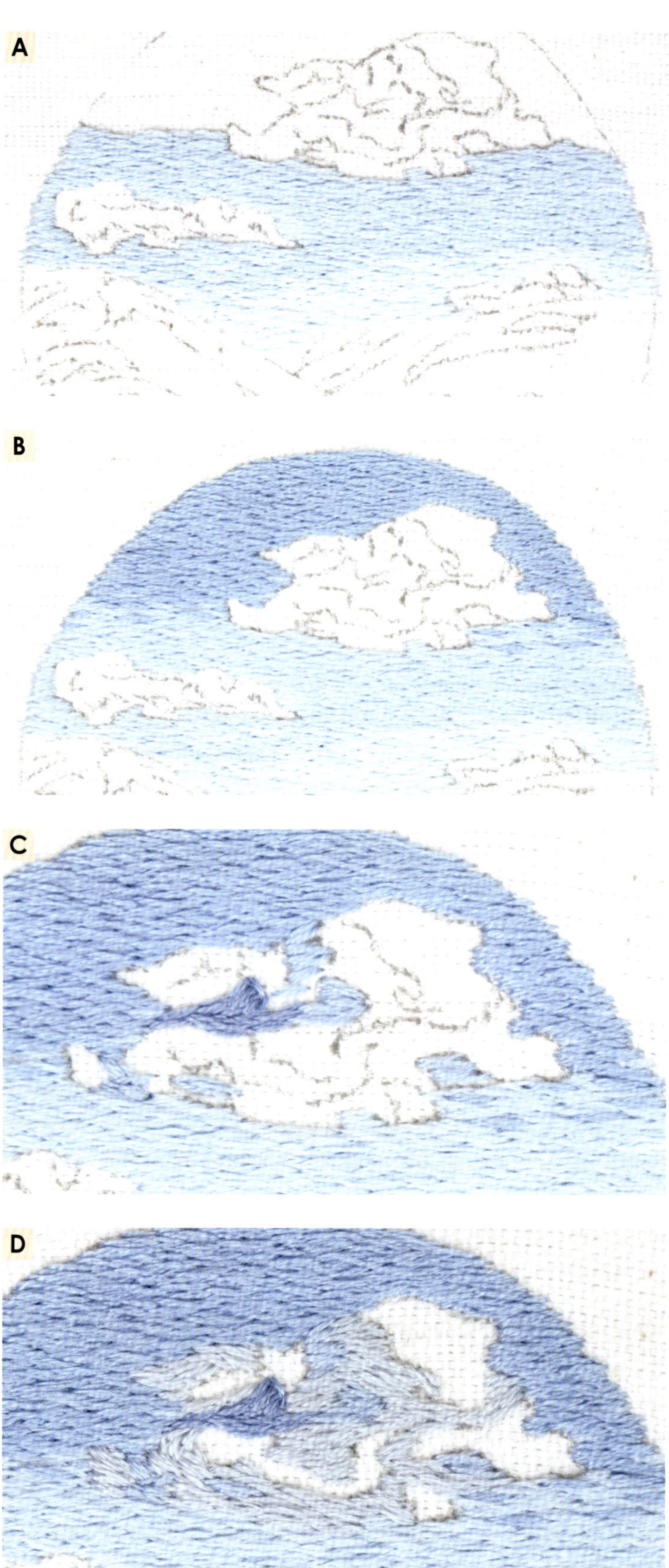

2. Shade with long and short stitches and seed stitches of 3753. Introduce 762 to fill the remaining gaps. **E** **F**

3. Blend accent seed stitches of BLANC along the top of the cloud and over the 762 sections. Blend 1 strand of 334 seed stitches into 3755 and near the top border. Blend split back stitches through the center of the cloud. Use 1 strand of BLANC to make small seed stitch highlights on the left side of the cloud. **G**

4. Begin filling the medium cloud to the left with long and short stitches and seed stitches of 3752. Shade in 3753, sloping downward on the right side of the cloud. **H**

Creating the Bumps

When creating the bumps of clouds, I find it easiest to stitch along the border first, then work inward to fill in the rest.

E

F

G

H

5. Layer in 762 with long and short stitches and seed stitches to fill the rest of the space in the cloud. I

6. Use 1 strand of 3755 to shade around 762 and across the cloud with seed stitches. Use 1 strand of 334 to seed stitch over the bottom of the cloud. J

7. Begin filling the small cloud to the right with seed stitches of 3752. Fill under the bump on the right, then shade the left side. Blend in 3753 seed stitches. Then, use the same color to fill the center of the cloud. K

8. Fill the 2 bumps at the top with seed stitches of 762. Add accent stitches to the left side of the cloud with 1 strand of 3755. L

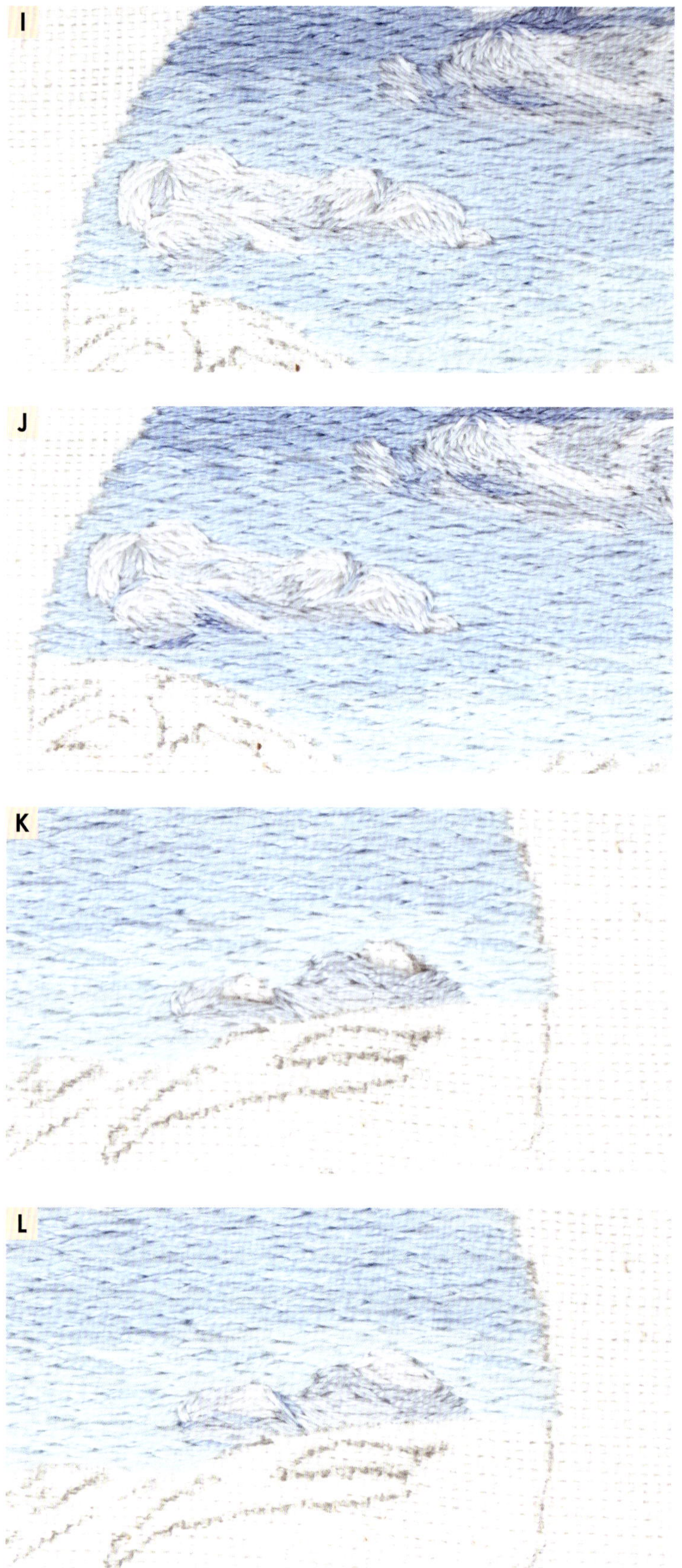

Hills: Background

1. Begin filling the center background hill with 926 angled long and short stitches. Add angled stitches as you blend. Continue with 320, then fill the remaining spaces with 18. A

2. Layer in straight stitches and seed stitches of 989. Use 1 strand of 3768 to split back stitch above the 926 section and blend in straight stitches. B

Hills: Middleground

1. Begin filling the left border of the left hill. Curve long and short stitches of 3346 down the hill. Blend and fill 470 down the hill. Blend in 471 down the left border. C D

Maintaining A Circular Border

As you work, the stitches might start warping the outer border of the design. To maintain a circular design, occasionally check the tautness of the base fabric and restretch it around the edges as needed.

2. Shade and fill the open spaces on the right slope of the hill using long and short stitches of 166. Then, fill in the rest of the hill with 18. E

3. Use 1 strand of 307 to blend long and short stitches down the left side of the 18 stitches. Accent the bottom right corner and center of the section. F

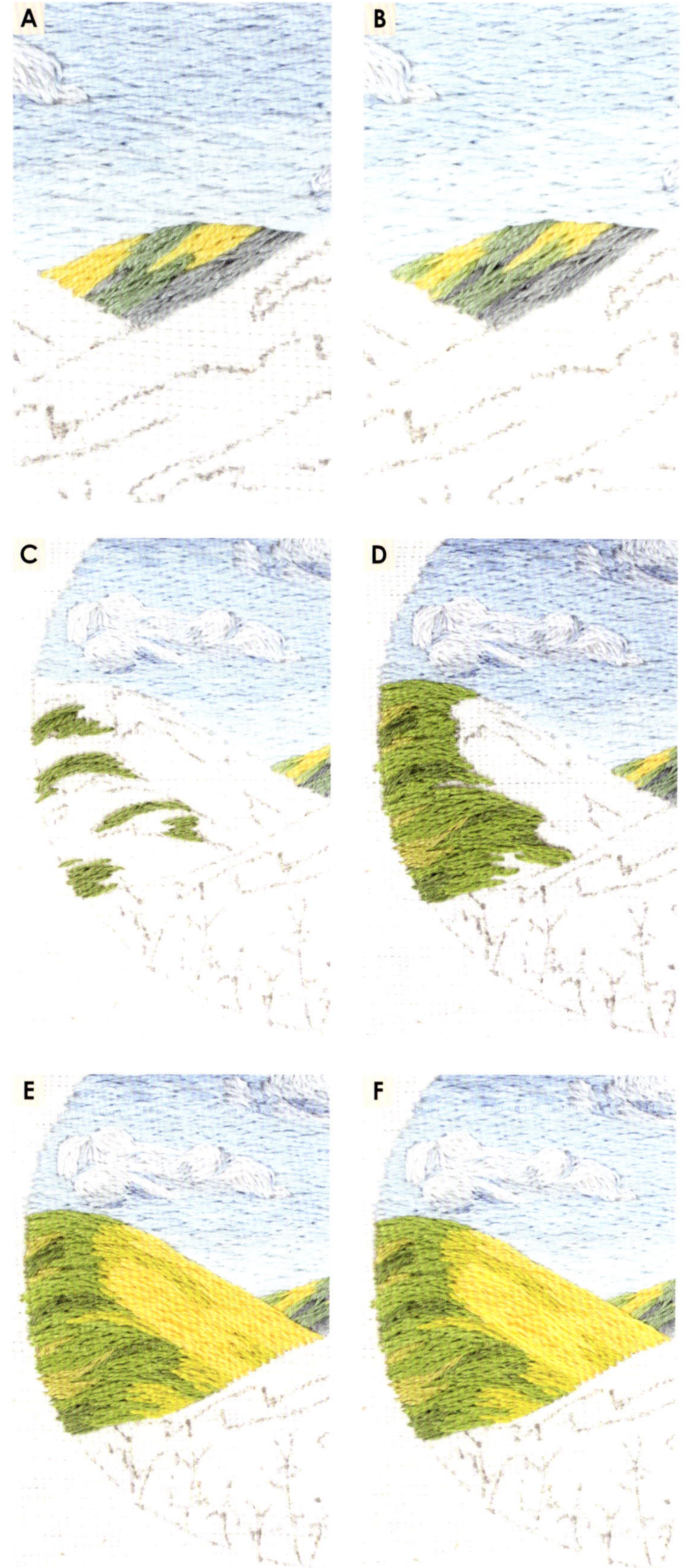

Hills: Foreground

1. Use 3346 to split back stitch and seed stitch the center of the hill. Use 1 strand of the same color to split back stitch the lower half of the foreground stems so they are easier to add to later. A

2. Use 3345 seed stitches to shade between the bumps of the flower bushes. Blend in long and short stitches of 3346. Add another patch higher on the hill and near the right border. B

3. Blend long and short stitches of 470 across the main part of the hill, leaving a gap in the center. Blend in 166 long and short stitches on the right side and center. Add a small section at the top right. C

4. Blend in a patch of 973 long and short stitches near the top of the hill. Fill the remaining open spaces with 307 long and short stitches. D

A

B

C

D

5. Blend in seed stitches of 166 across the center of the hill. Use 471 long and short stitches and seed stitches to shade into the center and bottom left. **E**

Flowers

1. Use 1 strand of 3346 to split back stitch the top halves of the foreground stems. Fill the bottom of the design with 973 seed stitches overlapping at various angles, covering the bottom halves of the stems. Sprinkle 1-stranded 307 stab stitches above the top edges of the 973 flower bushes. **A**

2. Restitch the bottom half of the flower stems with 1 strand of 3346. Use 1 strand of 307 to make single-loop and double-loop French knot flowers at the ends of the stems. **B**

E

A

B

SKILL LEVEL: BEGINNER

SEAGRASS SHORE

Seascapes are some of my favorite scenes to embroider because the color palette is so soothing, and the stitch paths are full of gentle curves. The addition of crashing waves and jagged rocks can add a touch of drama to this otherwise peaceful panorama. Inspired by family vacations along the coast, this project incorporates sky, sand, grass, and wave landscape elements *(see Landscape Element Tutorials, page 30).*

TOOLS & MATERIALS

- 5″ (12.7cm) embroidery hoop
- 3.74″ (9.5cm) Nurge Flexi Hoop (optional)
- Tapestry needle, size 26
- Embroidery scissors
- Seagrass Shore Pattern (page 158)
- 7″ × 7″ (17.8 × 17.8cm) square of natural-colored cotton duck canvas
- DMC six-stranded cotton embroidery floss (colors below)

COLOR GUIDE

TRANSFERRING THE PATTERN

Transfer the design onto the center of the 7″ × 7″ (17.8 × 17.8cm) fabric square (see Transferring Designs, page 17). Secure the fabric in the 5″ (12.7cm) working hoop.

STITCHING

Use 2 strands of thread unless otherwise noted.

DMC THREAD COLORS

			762	3753	3752	924	3768	926
503	927	3072	BLANC	03	648	04	842	543
3866	841	898	433	420	3046	372	524	731

Sky

1. Fill in the sky with a gradient of long and short stitches in 762, 3753, and 3752, working from the horizon line to the top of the design. Use straight stitches to blend the bands of color together. A

A

Covering Guidelines

You will cover some pattern lines as you embroider this design. Refer back to a picture of the pattern when it comes time to go back and stitch those parts.

Ocean

1. Use long and short stitches and seed stitches of 924 to create the structure for 5 wave bumps. Blend in seed stitches and long and short stitches of 3768. Then, switch to split back stitch as you continue across to the right side. **A**

2. Blend 3768 long and short stitches into the waves at the left side. Fill in the upper portion of the ocean with long and short stitches in 926. Then, shade down into the Step 1 area and toward the shore with split back stitches and long and short stitches. **B**

3. Continue to shade with 926 near the right border. Blend long and short stitches of 503, 927, and 3072 to build the gradient heading toward the shore. **C**

4. Fill the whitewater near the shore with long and short stitches in BLANC. Fill the wave at the center of the ocean with overlapping seed and straight stitches in BLANC. Use 1 strand of BLANC to split back stitch the wave crests. **D**

5. Shade the open space below the BLANC whitewater with long and short stitches of 03. Then, fill the last space with long and short stitches of 648. Use 1 strand of 3753 to accent the 3072 stitches. Use 1 strand of 04 split back stitches to line below the BLANC whitewater. **E**

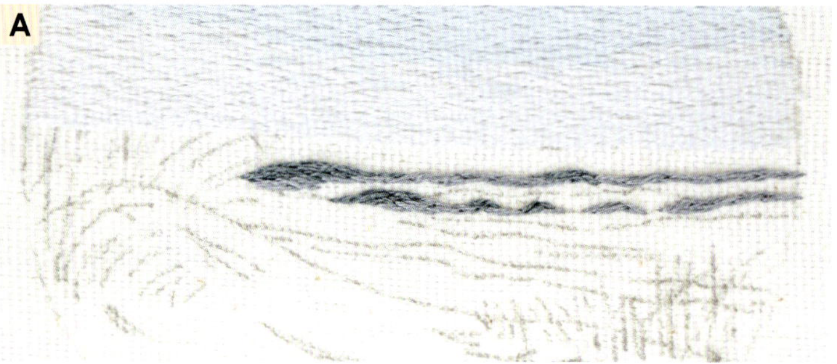
A

B

C

D

E

Sand Dune

1. Fill the dark patches of the sand dune with long and short stitches and straight stitches of 04 and 03. Blend a larger patch of 03 on the right side. Blend in long and short stitches of 842, filling the bottom border. A

2. Blend in long and short stitches of 543 and 3866 to fill the rest of the open space. B

3. Use 1 strand of 841 to edge split back stitches below the 04 and 03 patches. Use 1 strand of 543 to split back stitch the bottom of the 04 patches on the right. Blend 1-stranded seed stitches of 543 into the lower 842 stitches. C

Grass: Large Patch

Use 1 strand for this entire section.

1. Use 898, 433, and 420 split back stitches and seed stitches to add grass blades that curve up and right, overlapping them and varying where they come out of the ground. Refer to the pattern as needed or desired. D

2. Continue layering more grass with split back stitches in 3046, 372, and 524. Add short seed stitches of 731 and 420 at the base of the main patch. E

A

B

C

D

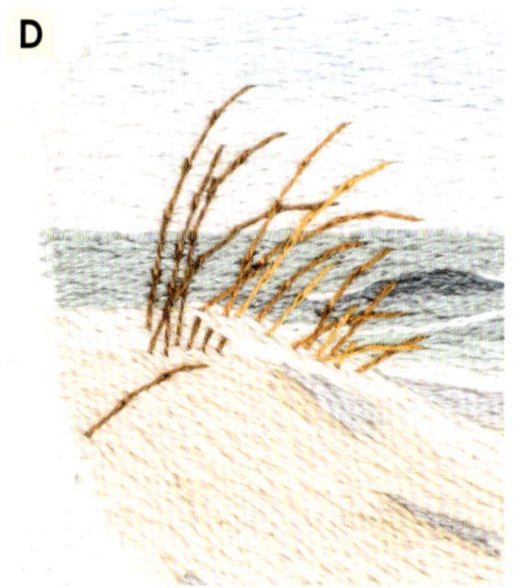

E

3. Layer more grass with split back stitches in 433, 420, 3046, 372, and 524. Expand the patch to the left border, varying the angles and curves. The grass should be tallest near the left border, and shortest as it recedes into the background. F G

4. Add small seed stitches of 731 at the base of the grass. Layer long, curved grass with split back stitches in 3866. Use 433, 420, and 3046 to create a smaller grass patch below. Blend seed stitches of 372 and 731 into the base to thicken the patch. Add 2 long blades of 3866. H

Grass: Medium Patch

Use 1 strand for this entire section.

1. Use a combination of seed stitches and split back stitches in 898 to create the base layer of grass blades. Layer 433 grass blades over. A

2. Use split back stitches in 372 to layer more grass. Add seed stitches in 731 to the base of the patch. B

3. Layer in blades of 3866, curving them out the right side of the frame. C

F

G

H

A

B

C

Grass: Small Patch

Use 1 strand for this entire section.

1. Use a combination of seed stitches and split back stitches in 898 to create the base layer of grass blades. Layer 433 and 420 grass blades over. **A**

2. Layer in blades of 372. Add 731 seed stitches into the base of the patch. **B**

3. Layer in 3 longer blades of 3866. **C**

A

B

C

ROCKY SEASCAPE

Seascapes that contain rock elements form a nice balance by including both smooth and rough surfaces. Including a large rock formation also creates a focal point that your eye is immediately drawn to, which helps produce a natural flow to your composition. Based on a photo I took at Morro Rock Beach, this project incorporates sky, rock, wave, and sand landscape elements (see Landscape Element Tutorials, page 30).

TOOLS & MATERIALS

- 5″ (12.7cm) embroidery hoop
- 3″ (7.6cm) display hoop (optional)
- 5″ × 5″ (12.7 × 12.7cm) shadow box (optional)
- Tapestry needle, size 26
- Embroidery scissors
- Rocky Seascape Pattern (page 158)
- 7″ × 7″ (17.8 × 17.8cm) square of natural-colored cotton duck canvas
- DMC six-stranded cotton embroidery floss (colors below)

COLOR GUIDE

TRANSFERRING THE PATTERN

Transfer the design onto the center of the 7″ × 7″ (17.8 × 17.8cm) fabric square (see Transferring Designs, page 17). Secure the fabric in the 5″ (12.7cm) working hoop.

STITCHING

Use 2 strands of thread unless otherwise noted.

DMC THREAD COLORS

								3753
162	827	3755	823	336	3750	930	3768	931
813	451	646	04	03	05	452	501	642
520	987	3346	3051	470	3345	3810	597	927
502	926	3841	318	BLANC	3809	932	06	3033

Sky

Fill the sky with horizontal long and short stitches of 3753, 162, 827, and 3755, stitching from the horizon line to the top of the design. Blend with horizontal straight stitches to create a smooth gradient. A

Rock Formation: Right Side

1. Following the detailed lines of the pattern, use seed and straight stitches of 823 and 336 to create the darkest parts of the rocks. B C

Angled Stitches

I find that adding stitches at varying angles really helps create a realistic, rocky texture.

2. Use 3750 seed stitches to shade into the existing areas. Use 930 seed stitches to shade the lone rock on the right, then accent and shade around the main rock. Use 3768 seed stitches and long and short stitches to fill the lone rock and blend into the existing shadows. D E

3. Use 931, 813, and 451 seed stitches and long and short stitches to begin filling the right side of the rock. Overlap 646 seed stitches between the 451 patches. F

4. Use overlapping seed stitches of 04, 03, and 05 to fill in the majority of the remaining space. Use 05 for the small rocks at the base of the cliff. G

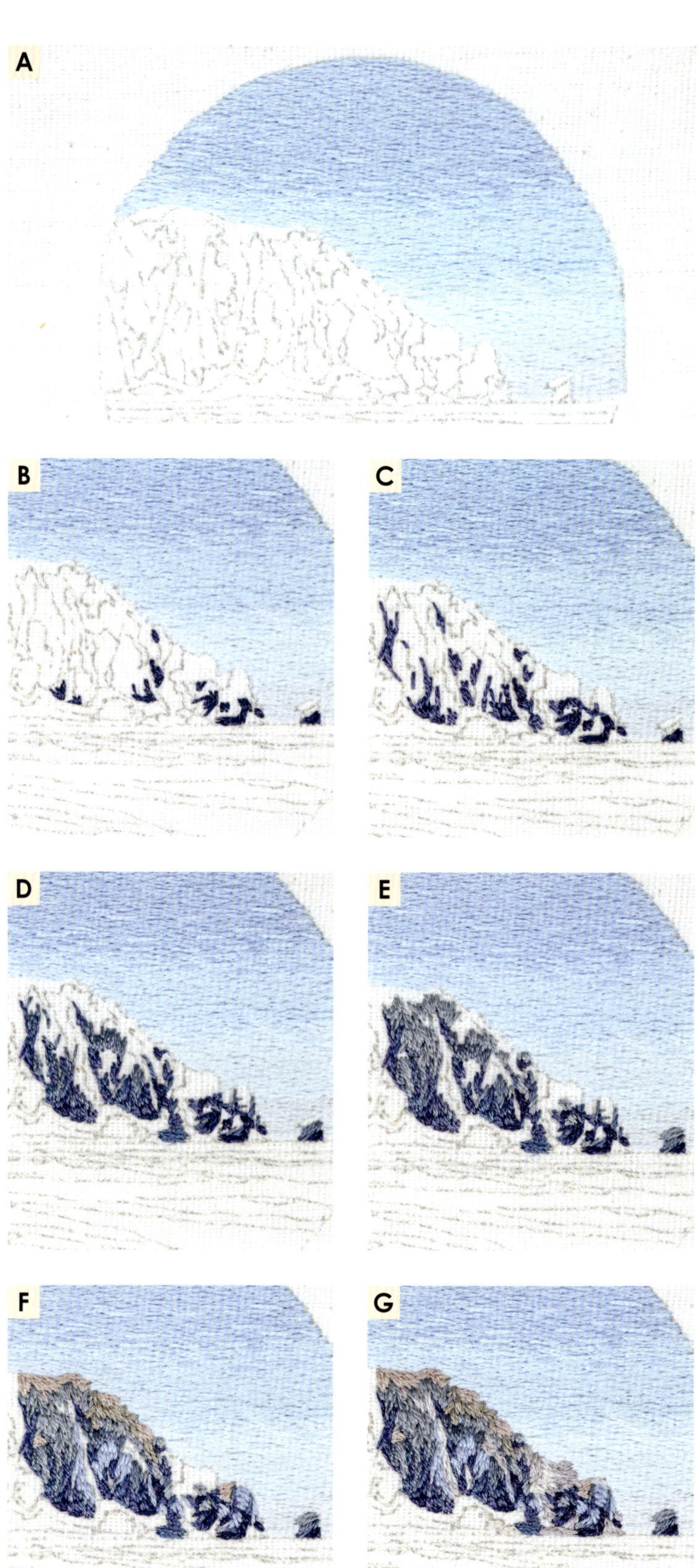

5. Use 1 strand of 336 to accent seed stitch across the cliff, following the Color Guide. Use 1 strand of 3768 to stab stitch over the 451 stitches at the top. Use 1 strand of 03 to stab and seed stitch across the cliff. H

6. Use 1 strand of 3768 to shade the bottoms of the 3 rocks at the base of the cliff. Use 1 strand of 930 to blend small seed stitches into the 931 stitches on the right. Use 1 strand of 452 to seed stitch the 451 at the top of the cliff. I

Rock Formation: Left Side

1. Following the detailed lines of the pattern, use split back stitches and seed stitches in 823 and 336 to create the dark vertical lines in the rocks. Blend in 3750 and 930 seed stitches (following that color order). A B

2. Shade in 3768 seed stitches and long and short stitches to begin filling the cliff face. Blend overlapping 501 seed stitches into the bottom left corner. Then, blend in 451 long and short stitches to fill near the top of the rock and connect to the right side. C

3. Blend in 646 seed stitches and long and short stitches in the upper right. Then use 04 long and short stitches and seed stitches to fill and blend across the cliff. Use 452 long and short stitches to fill near the left border. D

4. Use satin stitches and seed stitches in 452 to add patches and blend into the bottom right side. Use seed stitches of 642 to fill in, blending with the existing colors. Use 646 seed stitches for the 2 small remaining patches near the center. E

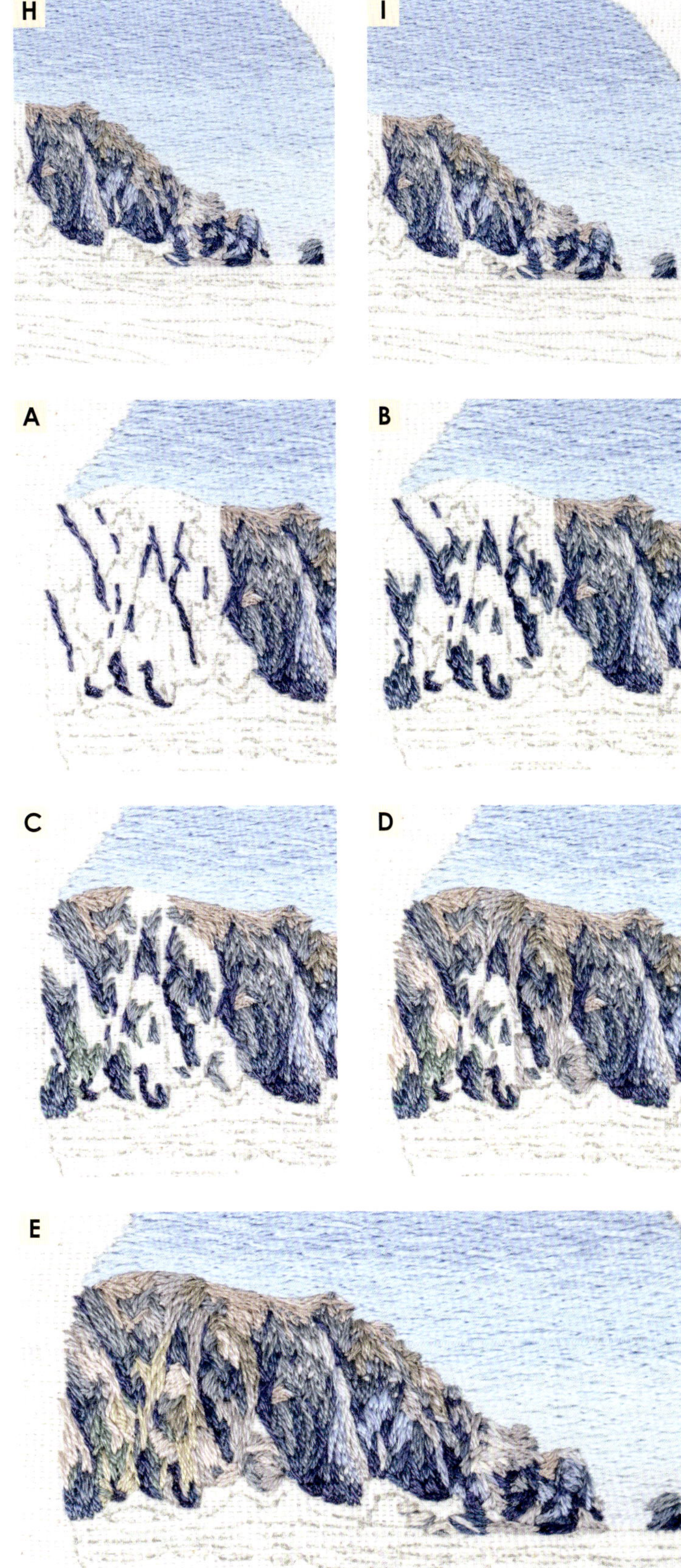

5. Use 1 strand of 336 seed stitches and straight stitches to create dark shadow lines on the cliff. Use 1 strand of 930 to blend seed stitches into the top of the rock and 452 patches. Shade the bottom right with 930 accent straight stitches. F

6. Use 1 strand of 05 to seed stitch in the upper right and bottom right corners of the section. Then, layer in accent seed and stab stitches across the cliff. G

Rock Formation: Greenery

1. Fill in patches of long and short stitches of 823, 520, and 987 across the bottom of the cliff. A

2. Blend in overlapping 3346 seed stitches and long and short stitches. Use 3051 long and short stitches to fill across the area. B

3. Fill the remaining open spaces and layer with long and short stitches and seed stitches of 470 and 3345. C

F

G

A

B

C

4. Use 1 strand of 3346 to blend overlapping seed stitches up the rock formation. Blend 1-stranded straight stitches into the 470 patch. Use 1 strand of 987 to shade around the Step 1 patch of 823. **D**

5. Use long and short stitches of 3768 to fill the horizontal space above the ocean line. Shade the patch using 1 strand of 823 seed and stab stitches. Use 1 strand of 930 to seed stitch the same patch. Use 1 strand of 451 to blend straight and stab stitches into the same patch. Use 1 strand of 05 to stab stitch along the bottom of the cliff. **E**

Ocean

1. Create a thin line of overlapping 3768 straight stitches at the horizon line behind the lone rock. Starting from the far right corner, blend 3810 and 597 long and short stitches toward the rocks. Use 927 long and short stitches to begin blending and adding across the ocean. Then, blend in 501 and 502. **A**

2. Use 926 long and short stitches to blend widely across the water. Then, blend in 597 long and short stitches. Blend in 3841 long and short stitches across the right, leaving room for whitewater. **B**

3. Blend in long and short stitches of 502, 926, 451, and 04. **C**

D

E

A

B

C

4. Add 04 stitches to the bottom right. Blend in 318 long and short stitches. Fill the open space with 926 long and short stitches, again leaving space for whitewater. **D**

5. Use BLANC long and short stitches to create whitewater and wave crests. Switch to 1 strand and use seed stitches to highlight below the lone rock. Then, highlight the whitewater around the upper and right 501 patches. Use the same thread to create broken lines of small waves between the whitewater. **E**

6. Use 1 strand of 3809 to straight stitch below the lone rock. Use 1 strand of 502 to split back stitch across the middle of the BLANC patch on the left, and straight stitch between the whitewater of the upper waves. Blend straight stitches into the 501 patch near the right border. **F**

7. Use 1 strand of 3841 to blend straight stitches into the 597 patch near the center, stitching to meet the whitewater. Add straight stitches around the 451 patch on the left. Use 1 strand of 932 to stitch across the 926 patch. Use 1 strand of 3768 to shade below the foreground whitewater with seed stitches. **G**

D

E

F

G

Shore

1. Fill the upper portion of the shore with long and short stitches in 451. Use 1 strand of BLANC to stitch the bubbling water around it. Then, switch back to 451 and continue stitching below the BLANC bubble line. Split back stitch to re-establish the bubble line with 1 strand of BLANC. **A**

2. Blend in long and short stitches of 04 and 932. Use 1 strand of BLANC to split back stitch over the bubble line on the right. **B**

3. Shade in long and short stitches of 452. Shade in long and short stitches of 05. Then, switch to 1 strand and blend the 2 patches together. **C**

4. Fill in long and short stitches of 06 and 3033 to finish the shore. **D**

A

B

C

D

SKILL LEVEL: INTERMEDIATE

SERENE LAGOON

Landscapes that have a lot of small details are fun to embroider because you get to see the piece slowly come to life with each embellishment. When embroidering an intricate piece, it's easy to get carried away with the number of thread colors you use, but the final product is usually the better for it. Inspired by childhood memories exploring creeks and ponds, this project incorporates sky, mountain, tree, flower, grass, and calm water landscape elements (see Landscape Element Tutorials, page 30).

TOOLS & MATERIALS

- 5″ (12.7cm) embroidery hoop
- 3″ (7.6cm) display hoop and 3″ (7.6cm) square Modern Hoopla frame (optional)
- Tapestry needle, size 26
- Embroidery scissors
- Serene Lagoon Pattern (page 158)
- Hoop stand (optional, but recommended)
- 7″ × 7″ (17.8 × 17.8cm) square of natural-colored cotton duck canvas
- DMC six-stranded cotton embroidery floss (colors below)

COLOR GUIDE

TRANSFERRING THE PATTERN

Transfer the design onto the center of the 7″ × 7″ (17.8 × 17.8cm) fabric square (see Transferring Designs, page 17). Secure the fabric in the 5″ (12.7cm) working hoop.

STITCHING

Use 2 strands of thread unless otherwise noted.

DMC THREAD COLORS

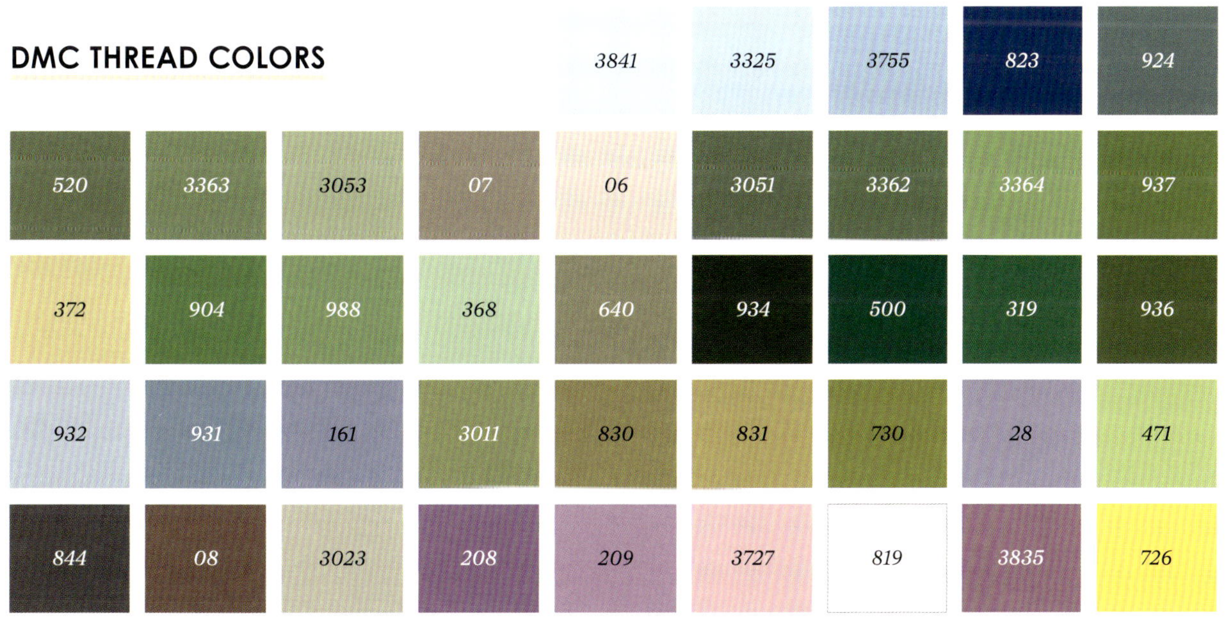

Sky

Fill the sky with horizontal long and short stitches, blending with straight stitches to create a smooth gradient. Begin with 3841 across the bottom of the sky. Blend in 3325 for the middle of the sky, and 3755 for the top of the sky. **A**

Covering Guidelines

The guidelines for the tops of the trees on the right will be lost as you embroider this design. Refer back to the pattern as needed.

Mountains: Back

1. Shade and blend the small patches of the mountain on the right with seed stitches of 823, 924, and 520 (following that color order). Then, use 520 long and short stitches to shade down the slope. **B**

2. Fill in the majority of the open space with 3363 long and short stitches. Use 3053 long and short stitches for the remaining small area at the center top. **C**

3. Use 1 strand of 3053 to add accent seed stitches. Use 1 strand of 07 to blend straight and seed stitches into the 3363 patches. Use 1 strand of 823 to stab stitch and split back stitch final details. **D**

Mountains: Front

1. Use seed stitches of 823 to begin filling patches on the central mountain. Blend in 924 seed stitches. Then create patches of satin stitches, long and short stitches, and seed stitches of 520. **E**

2. Use long and short stitches, satin stitches, and seed stitches of 3363 to begin filling the left side of the mountain and blending with the 520 patches. Fill the remaining space at the top left of the mountain with satin stitches and long and short stitches of 07. F

3. Use 1 strand of 924 to split back stitch and accent seed stitch the left side of the mountain. Use 1 strand of 823 to add accent stab stitches. Use 1 strand of 06 to accent stab stitch the 07 patch. G

4. Use long and short stitches and seed stitches of 520 to travel down the center of the mountain and blend with the existing patches at the lower right. Add a cluster of seed stitches. H

5. Blend long and short stitches of 3363 in between the 520 patches on the left. Then, fill the majority of the open space on the right. Blend into the stitches on the back mountain. Fill the remaining spaces with long and short stitches of 3053 and 07. I

6. Use 1 strand of 520 to split back stitch a ridge line. Then, blend in seed stitches to the 3363 patch on the right. Use 1 strand of 924 to blend straight and seed stitches across the center of the mountain and into the 07 patches. Finally, use 1 strand of 06 to stab stitch below the left 07 patch. J

Foothill

1. Fill the majority of the foothill with long and short stitches of 3051, paying attention to the stitch direction. Avoid covering the small tree guidelines, and fill the bottom right area with long and short stitches of 3362. Then, fill the remaining top area with long and short stitches of 3364. A

2. Use 1 strand of 937 to blend straight stitches into the 3051 patches. Use 1 strand of 372 to accent seed stitch the top of the hill. Use 1 strand of 3362 to stab stitch the 3364 patch. Use 1 strand of 823 to stab stitch across the hill. B

Meadow

1. Use long and short stitches and straight stitches of 520 and 904 to blend horizontal patches across the meadow and bank, following the Color Guide. Use seed stitches to overlap and blend. C D

2. Blend in large patches of long and short stitches in 937. Then, blend in 988 long and short stitches to fill the remaining largest spaces. Shade the space to the right of the tree with long and short stitches of 368. E

A

B

C

D

E

3. Use 1 strand of 937 to add straight stitches and seed stitches, blending between the greens above the water. Use 1 strand of 640 to blend seed stitches into the curvy area of 988 on the right. F

Trees

Use 1 strand for this entire section. Make single-loop French knots any time French knots or knots are referenced.

1. Fill in the space at the base of the foothill with clusters of 520 French knots. Create the trunk of the large tree on the left with 934 seed stitches. Then, embroider 2 dense French knot clusters in 500 to begin filling the tree. A

2. Continue filling the tree with more clusters of French knots. Use 319 for the bottom and left of the tree, then switch to 904. B

3. Fill the remaining space of the tree with 988 French knots. Add 904 accent knots to the 500 cluster in the center of the tree, and to extend the existing 904 patches to the right. Scatter 3364 accent knots across the tree. C

4. On the right side, straight stitch in 934 to create 6 tree trunks. Use angled 934 seed stitches to add branches to each tree. D

5. Add 936 accent seed stitches on the left side of the trees. E

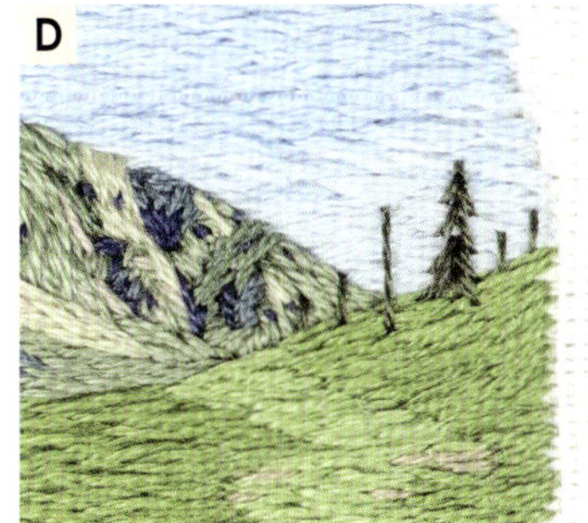

Water

1. Blend horizontal seed stitches of 823, 924, and 520 down from the upper center of the lagoon to create a reflection of the mountain. Use a combination of seed stitches and long and short stitches of 520 to begin filling the left side of the water. **A**

Mountain Reflection

When creating this calm body of water, keeping the stitches horizontal will give a more realistic impression of a reflection.

2. Blend 3363 and 07 seed stitches into the center reflection to fill the open space. Use 1 strand of 934 to add seed stitches and straight stitches where the meadow meets the water. **B**

3. Blend patches of 932, 931, 161, and 3011 long and short stitches down the water toward the bottom of the design, following the Color Guide. **C**

4. Blend in patches of 830, 831, 730, and 28 to fill in the water above the foreground reeds. **D**

5. Use 3051 long and short stitches to fill the remaining open space at the bottom, only leaving gaps for the rocks. **E**

6. Use 1 strand of 471 to blend seed stitches into the 831 patch. Use 1 strand of 931 to blend straight stitches across the lower portion of the water. Use 1 strand of 932 to blend straight stitches throughout the water. Use 1 strand of 936 to add seed stitches along the edges of the water. **F**

Rocks

1. Fill the right rock with overlapping straight stitches and seed stitches of 844, 08, and 3023. Add straight stitches of 936 below the rock. **G**

2. Fill the left rock with overlapping seed stitches of 844, 08, and 3023. **H**

Flowers

Use 1 strand for this entire section.

1. Add lots of stab stitches in 208 across the meadow. On the left, follow the curved line of 904 stitching, lessening in density as you move down from the line. On the right, follow the 937 patch, then create a few dense clusters across the field. Create a few larger flowers near the water with small seed stitches. Sprinkle 209 stab stitches across all the flowers, and add small 208 seed stitches to the larger flowers. **A** **B**

E

F

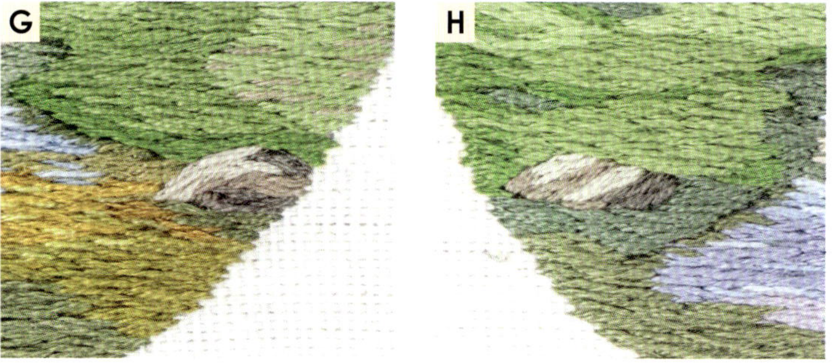
G H

A

B

2. Use stab stitches in 3727 to add flowers below the tree on the left. Layer 819 stab stitches on top, then spread them out further across the meadow. Use 3835 to add stab stitches to the shade below the large tree and near the right border. C

3. Use 3835 to embroider flowers across the foreground at the base of the design by angling 2–3 seed stitches together. Vary the flowers in size, creating some with just stab stitches. Highlight with 3727 seed stitches. D

4. Use 819 straight stitches and seed stitches to create 10 larger flowers. Angle and cross the stitches to look like daisies. Add a few pairs of parallel seed stitches. Add 726 stab stitches to the centers of the flowers. E

Grass

Use 1 strand for this entire section.

1. Starting at the top of the water, use 904 to add vertical seed stitches densely along the left bank of the lagoon. A

Reworking Grass

Because the guidelines have all been covered, you have some creative freedom in placing the blades of grass. Refer to the pattern as desired, but stitch the angle, source, and number of blades at your discretion.

C

D

E

A

2. Blend small seed stitches in 988 into the top of the 904 grass and across the meadow. Repeat Steps 1–2 across the top and right of the lagoon bank. B C

3. Use overlapping straight stitches and seed stitches in 934 to shade the foreground. D

4. Blend 904 straight stitches into the grass from Step 3. Add a few more blades to the right. Add 988 accent stitches across the foreground. E

B

C

D

E

SKILL LEVEL: INTERMEDIATE

FOOTHILL LAKE

Scenes that include multiple textures keep the eye moving across the piece. The French knot work in the trees and the wide range of colors makes this piece come alive. Inspired by artist William Mellor (1851–1931) and childhood trips to Cachuma Lake and Red Rock pools, this project incorporates sky & cloud, hill, tree, and calm water elements (see Landscape Element Tutorials, page 30).

TOOLS & MATERIALS

- 5″ (12.7cm) embroidery hoop
- 3″ (7.6cm) display hoop (optional) and 3″ (7.6cm) square Modern Hoopla frame (optional)
- Tapestry needle, size 26
- Embroidery scissors
- Foothill Lake Pattern (page 159)
- Hoop stand (recommended)
- 7″ × 7″ (17.8 × 17.8cm) square of natural-colored cotton duck canvas
- DMC six-stranded cotton embroidery floss (colors below)

COLOR GUIDE

TRANSFERRING THE PATTERN

Transfer the design onto the center of the 7″ × 7″ (17.8 × 17.8cm) fabric square (see Transferring Designs, page 17). Secure the fabric in the 5″ (12.7cm) working hoop.

STITCHING

Use 2 strands of thread unless otherwise noted.

DMC THREAD COLORS

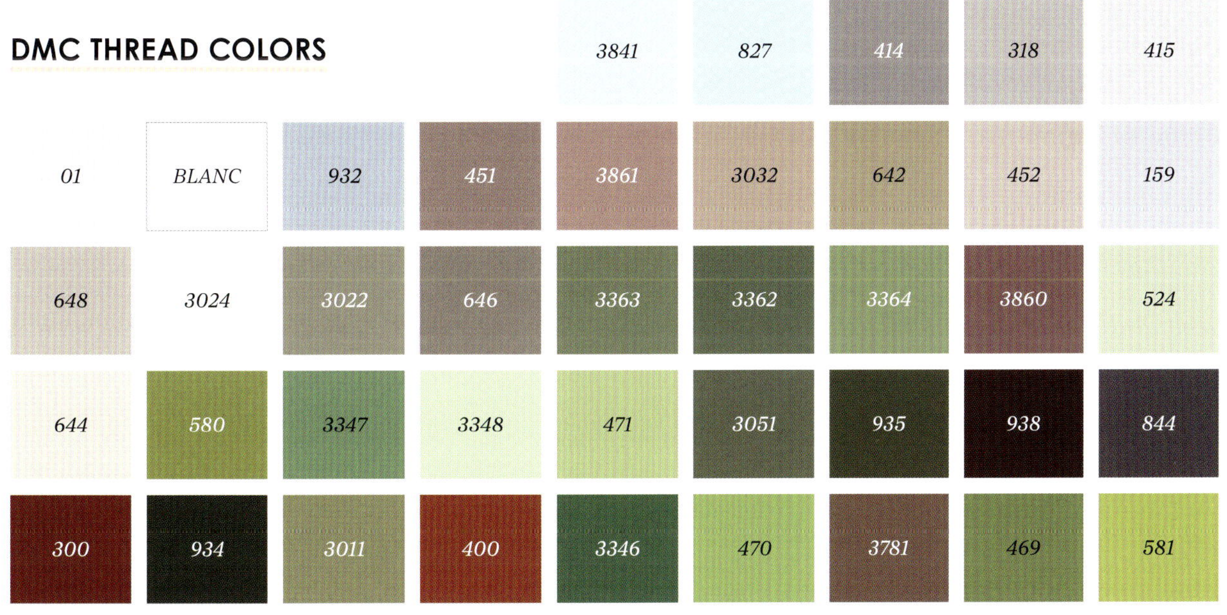

Sky

Use long and short stitches and seed stitches in 3841 to fill the bottom of the sky above the clouds. Then, blend in 827 long and short stitches to fill the top of the design. Blend the gradient with horizontal straight stitches. **A**

Clouds

1. Use long and short stitches and straight stitches of 414 across the cloud from left to right, following the Color Guide. Blend in long and short stitches and seed stitches of 318, again moving from left to right. Repeat to blend in 415, filling most of the left side of the cloud, and beginning to add to the center. **B**

Cloud Texture

To create the rounded, puffy texture and dimension, place stitches to follow the curves of the pattern guidelines.

2. Continue filling with 415 to the right side of the cloud. Then, use 01 long and short stitches to fill the remaining open space. **C**

3. Use BLANC to accent across the clouds with seed stitches. Use 1 strand of 932 to blend into the 318 and 414 patches. **D** **E**

A

B

C

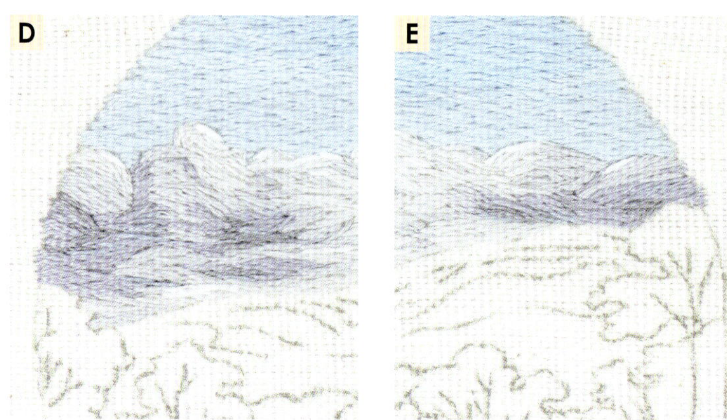

D E

Hill

1. Begin filling the hill with long and short stitches and seed stitches of 451 and 3861. Then, use 318 long and short stitches to fill the majority of the left side, center, and top right. Use split back stitches in the top right. **A**

2. Blend in long and short stitches of 3032, 642, 452, 159, and 3861 to fill the curving gaps in the hillside, leaving space open above the trees. Use 318 to shade to the right of the 3861 stitches. Line the upper right border of the 159 section with split back stitches. **B**

3. Use 1 strand of 648 to add accent straight stitches across the hill. Use 1 strand of 3024 to add seed stitch highlights on the right side of the hill. Use 1 strand of 414 to accent the 318 patches across the hill. Use 1 strand of 3022 to blend into the 318 stitches on the left and right. **C**

4. Use overlapping seed stitches of 646 to shade the small areas above the trees on the left and between the trees on the right. Then, shade in the majority of the space above the trees with long and short stitches of 3022. **D**

A

B

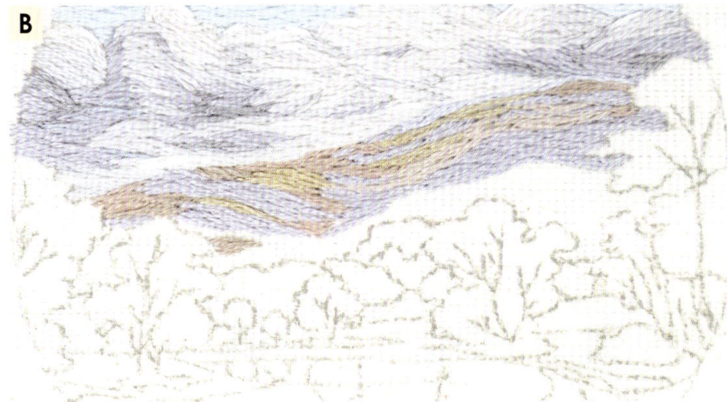

C

D

5. Fill the remaining space above the tree line with long and short stitches of 3363. Blend in accent seed stitches of the same color. **E**

6. Use 1 strand of 3362 to add seed and stab stitches to the 3363 patch. Use 1 strand of 3364 to blend seed stitches above the 3363 patch. Use 1 strand of 3860 to seed and stab stitch the 3363 patch. **F**

Grass: Background

1. Use long and short stitches and seed stitches in 451 to fill in background space around the tree trunks. Continue filling in with 3022, 524, 3861, and 644, following the pattern lines and Color Guide. **A**

2. Blend in stitches of 580 and 3347. Then, use 1 strand of 451 to add overlapping straight stitches from below the 580 patch to the right. Add straight stitches with 1 strand of 452 above the 644 patch. **B**

E

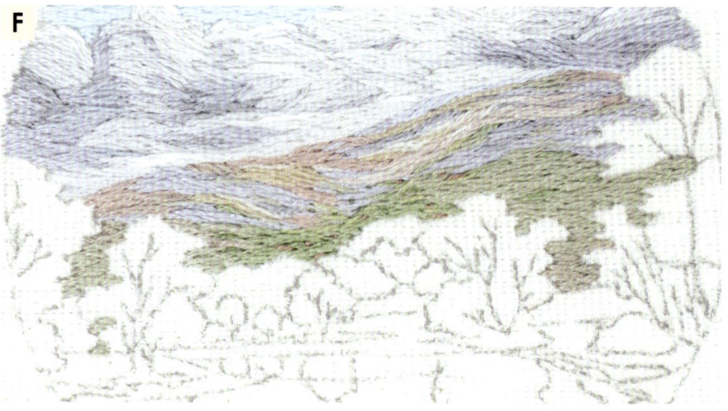
F

A

B

3. Use 1 strand of 3861 to extend the existing 3861 patch. Use 1 strand of 3860 to accent below the 580 patch. Shade the ground on the left with 2 strands of 3860. C

4. Layer seed stitches of 3347 above the 3860 patch. Long and short stitch the open space with 3348. Use 1 strand of 471 to blend seed stitches into the 3348 section. D

5. Fill in long and short stitches of 3861 at the bottom. Use 1 strand of 452 to blend over the 3861 patch and shade the space on the right. Use 1 strand of 644 and 3860 to accent the 3861 patch. E

6. Fill in long and short stitch patches of 3051, 471, and 3348 on the right side. F

C

D

E

F

7. Fill in the right border and bottom with long and short stitches and seed stitches of 580, 3347, and 935. G

8. Use 1 strand of 471 to blend straight stitches into the right side of the 3051 patch. Then, blend angled seed stitches into the 935 patches. H

Tree Trunks

Use 1 strand for this entire section.

1. Use split back stitches and seed stitches of 938 to stitch the trunks and branches of the trees on the left and right sides. Use 844 to stitch the small trees in the center. Use 300 to stitch the remaining tree at the center right. A B

Tree Trunk Placement

Because the tree trunk guidelines were partially lost when the grass and ground was created, refer to the pattern to stitch them.

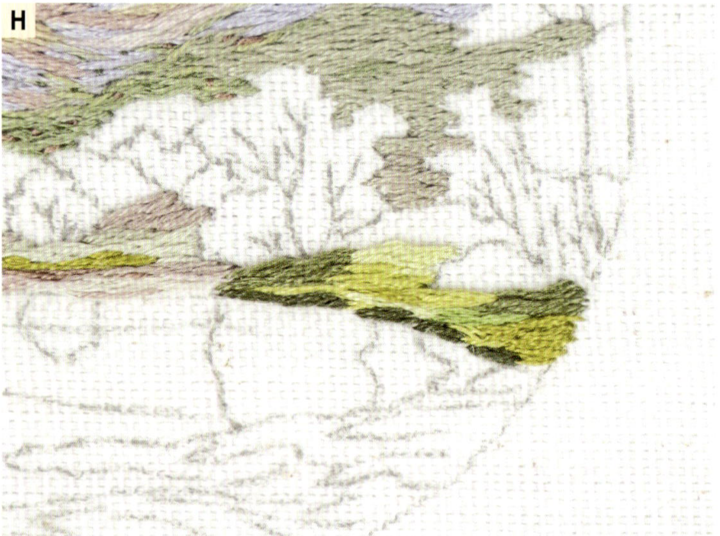

Trees: Background

Use 1 strand for this entire section. Make single-loop French knots anytime French knots or knots are referenced.

1. Create a gradient of French knots moving from the base of the background trees to the tops. Start with 934, then continue with 3362 and 3363. Use 3364 to fill the tops. A B

2. Add accent knots throughout the foliage on the right with 3051 and 938. C

3. Fill the background space on the left with 3011 French knots. Accent stab stitch the 3011 knots with 400. Fill the space on the right with 3051 and 3346 French knots. D E

4. Moving back to the three small trees in the center, shade and fill the foliage with 3346 and 3347 French knots. Accent the tops of the trees with 3348 knots. F

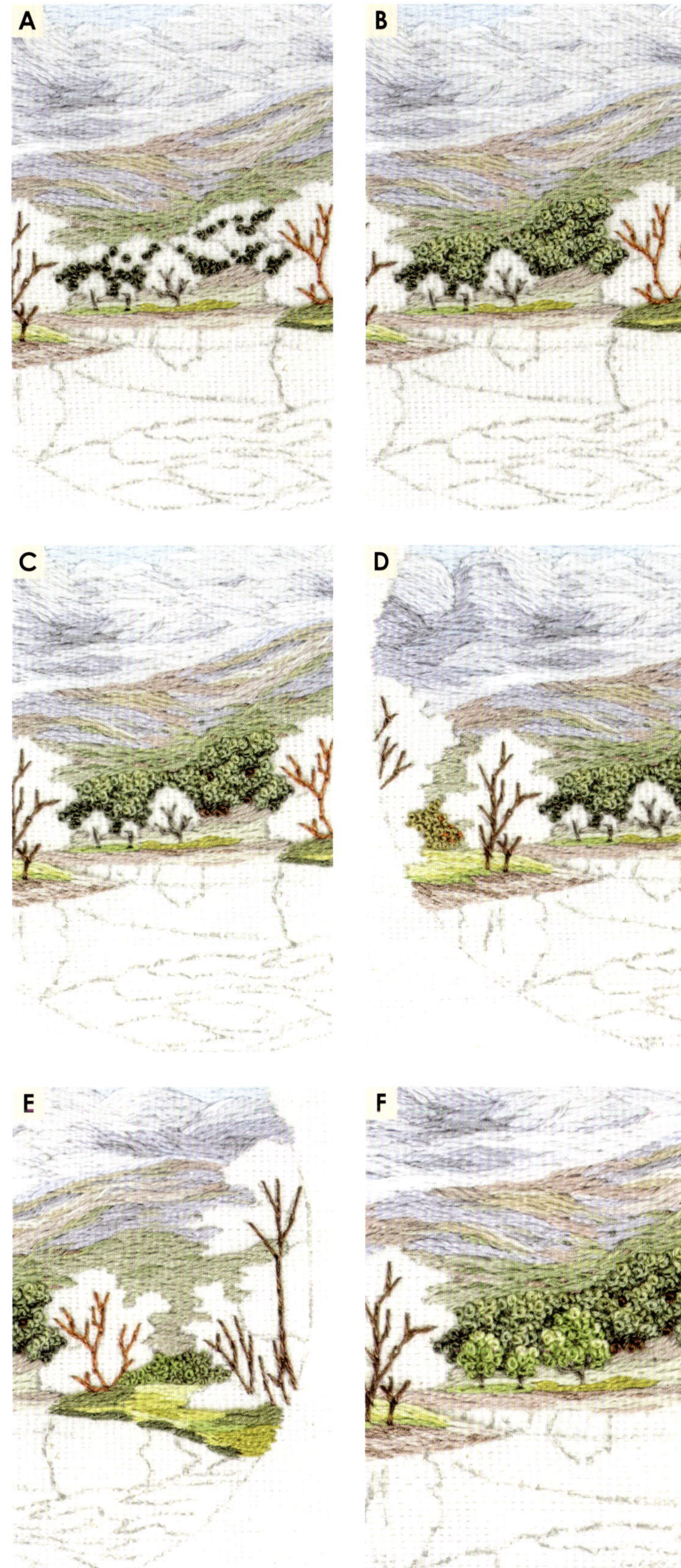

Trees: Middleground

Use 1 strand for this entire section. Make single-loop French knots anytime French knots or knots are referenced.

1. Use 3362 and 3346 French knots to fill in around the branches of the trees on the left. Shade the bush below with 3346 knots. A B

2. Use 580 French knots to fill the remaining spaces in the trees. Then, fill the bush below with 3347. Add accent knots of the same color to the trees. Accent the tops and right sides of the trees with 471 knots. C

3. Move to the center right tree. Use 3362, 3011, and 580 to densely cluster French knots up the tree on both sides of the trunk. D

4. Continue to fill the tree with 3346 and 3347 knots. Fill the top and accent with 471 French knots. E

5. Move to the lower far right tree. Use 580, 3347, and 470 French knots between the branches. Accent the top with 471 knots. Fill the right border with 3011 knots. F

Seed Stitches In Tight Spaces

Replace French knots with seed stitches when the knots might cover branches that you would like to remain exposed.

A

B

C

D

E

F

6. Shade up the remaining tree with French knots of 935, 3362, and 3011. G

7. Blend in 3346 French knots. Then, fill the upper and left sides of the tree with 580 and 3347 knots. Accent the upper half of the tree with 471 knots. H

8. Fill the small remaining bush with French knots in 935, 938, 300, 3346, and 580. Accent the top with 471 knots. I

Water

1. Covering the reflection guidelines of the small trees, fill large sections of the water, starting in the upper center, with long and short stitches of 318, 415, and 01. Use 1 strand of 3362 to shade tree reflections on top of the water with overlapping seed and straight stitches. Extend the reflections with 1 strand of 3363. A

2. Use 3362 straight stitches to shade a tree reflection on the left. Blend in long and short stitches of 3051 and 580 to fill the space. Use 1 strand of 938 to split back stitch tree trunk reflections. Use 1 strand of 3362 to add horizontal stitches across the trunks. **B**

3. Use 3011, 580, 3346, and 471 long and short stitches to blend the large tree reflection on the right. Use seed stitches of 3362 and 3347 to fill the tiny tree reflection on the far right. **C**

4. Use 1 strand of 415 to create a line across the center of the water with overlapping straight stitches. Blend horizontal straight stitches into the right side of the 01 patch to blend. Add seed stitches into the left tree reflection. **D**

5. Use 1 strand of 318 to seed stitch the sides of the right tree reflections. Use 1 strand of 300 to stitch the trunk reflection. Then, with 1 strand of 580, add a couple horizontal stitches across the trunks. **E**

B

C

D

E

Grass: Foreground

1. Use long and short stitches in 935, 3362, and 3051 across the foreground grass, following the pattern. Seed stitch with 935 at the top right. A

2. Blend in long and short stitches of 3781, 3051, 469, 3346, and 580 to continue filling in the space. B

3. Use 581 long and short stitches to fill the remaining open space. Seed stitch the upper 580 patch to blend. C

4. Use 1 strand of 3348 to split back stitch the top edge of the foreground grass. Seed stitch below. Use 1 strand of 3362 to blend seed stitches into the 580 and 581 patches. Use 1 strand of 580 to blend seed stitches into both sides of the lower 581 patch. D

SKILL LEVEL: ADVANCED

VINEYARD VALLEY

Creating rural landscapes that incorporate both pastoral and agricultural characteristics holds a special place in my heart. These places remind me of the areas neighboring my hometown of Santa Barbara. This vineyard scene uses color and scale to create depth, and French knot work to build dimension. Inspired by a day of wine tasting in Los Olivos, CA, this project incorporates sky & cloud, hill, tree, and flower elements (see Landscape Element Tutorials, page 30).

TOOLS & MATERIALS

- 5″ (12.7cm) embroidery hoop
- 3″ (7.6cm) display hoop (optional) and 3″ (7.6cm) circle Modern Hoopla frame (optional)
- Tapestry needle, size 26
- Chenille needle, size 26 (optional)
- Embroidery scissors
- Vineyard Valley Pattern (page 159)
- Hoop stand (recommended)
- Thimble (recommended)
- 7″ × 7″ (17.8 × 17.8cm) square of natural-colored cotton duck canvas
- DMC six-stranded cotton embroidery floss (colors below)

TRANSFERRING THE PATTERN

Transfer the design onto the center of the 7″ × 7″ (17.8 × 17.8cm) fabric square (see Transferring Designs, page 17). Secure the fabric in the 5″ (12.7cm) working hoop.

COLOR GUIDE

STITCHING

Use 2 strands of thread unless otherwise noted.

DMC THREAD COLORS

30	794	157	3836	761	3713	3753	26	341
23	04	646	3768	926	28	318	3023	648
3864	927	3041	841	738	437	3051	436	434
3828	422	435	739	890	3345	3346	3347	3364
988	989	470	581	580	3854	3853	501	3362
3363	520	471	934	3052	838	936	08	

Sky

1. Use long and short stitches of 30 and 794 to begin shading the right side of the sky. Use 30 split back stitches to create thinner lines to the right. **A**

Cloud Texture

Because these clouds have such subtle edges, it is important to angle your stitches to give the impression of wispy clouds. Smooth color blending is also important to this design.

2. Use long and short stitches and straight stitches of 157, 3836, and 761 to fill and blend color across the sky. Use seed stitches of 3836 on the right and left. **B**

3. Blend in long and short stitches of 3713 and 3753 to fill in the sky. Use 1 strand of 3753 to blend straight stitches into the 157 stitches on the right. **C**

4. Fill the remaining space at the top and majority of the left of the sky with long and short stitches of 26. Use long and short stitches of 341 to fill the small open space in the middle. Seed stitch near the left border. **D**

5. Use overlapping straight stitches and split back stitches in 23 to fill the remaining space on the left and highlight the clouds below. Use long and short stitches and seed stitches in the same color to highlight the clouds at the top. **E**

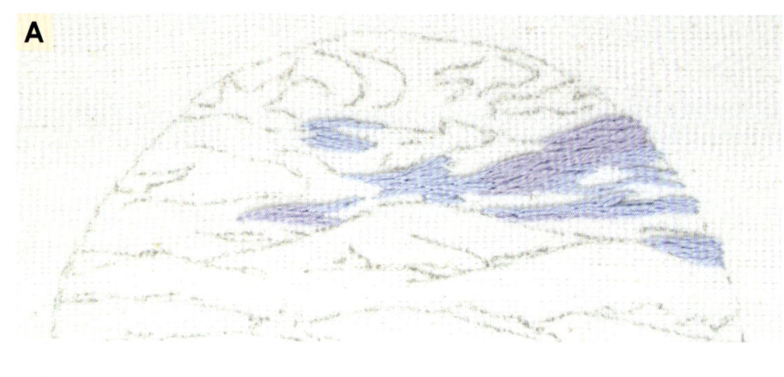
A

B

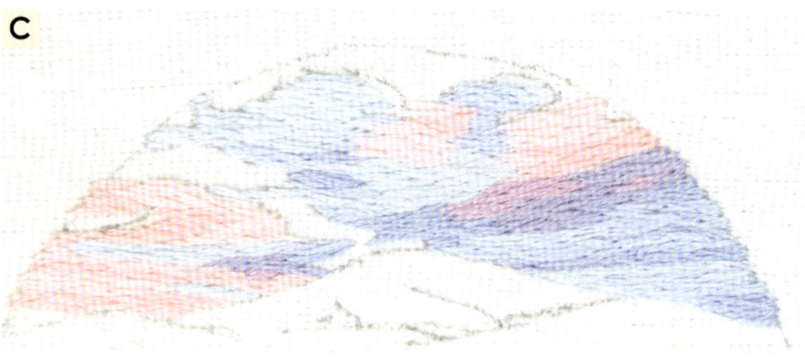
C

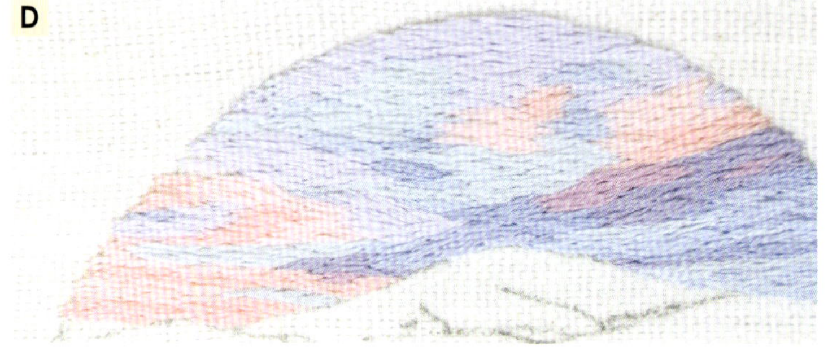
D

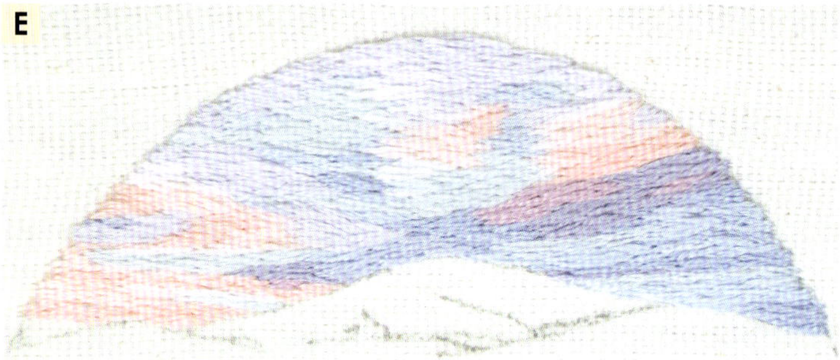
E

6. Use 1 strand of 3753 to blend straight stitches into the central 3753 patch. Use 1 strand of 157 to blend straight stitches into the bottom of the large 30 patch and the bottom of the same 3753 patch. **F**

7. Use 1 strand of 341 to accent stitch the bottom of the 26 patch at the lower left, blending it into the surrounding stitches. Use 1 strand of 3836 to accent near 341 stitches and the upper left of the sky with seed stitches. **G**

Hills: Background

1. Blend long and short stitches of 04 and 646 for the tallest central hill, leaving space for the trees. Below, shade with 28 and 318 long and short stitches and seed stitches. On the right, blend long and short stitches of 3768 and 926. Blend the same 2 colors on the left side. Fill in more 318 on the left side. **A**

2. Fill the largest remaining spaces in the central area with 3023 long and short stitches. Fill the left remaining area with 3023, 648, and 3864 long and short stitches. Line the tops of the hills with overlapping straight stitches of 648. **B** **C**

F

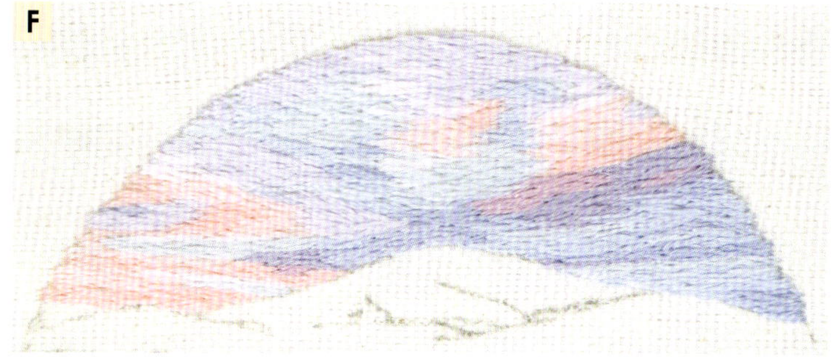

G

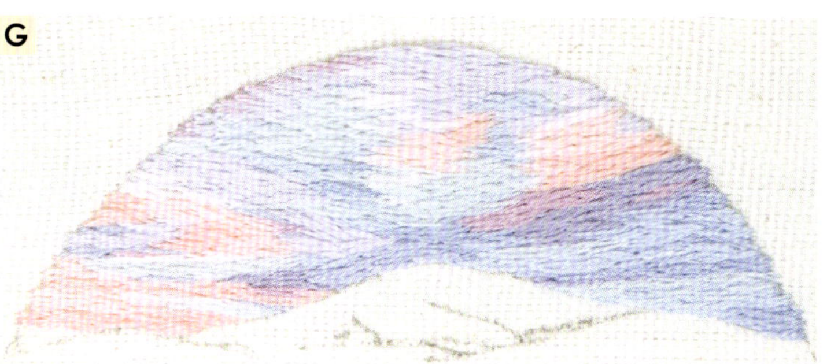

A

B

C

3. Use 1 strand of 927 to highlight the right hill with seed and straight stitches. Use 1 strand of 926 to blend the 926 patches in with the surrounding areas. Then, add accent seed stitches. D E

4. Use 1 strand of 318 to blend straight stitches between 3023 and 926 on the right. Add seed stitches to extend the 318 patch in the center. Use seed stitches to blend the existing 318 patches on the left with the surrounding areas. Use 1 strand of 3768 to seed stitch the center hill and blend the existing 3768 patch into the neighboring stitches. Use 1 strand of 646 to blend the top 646 patch with the surrounding areas. Blend small seed stitches into the 04 patch below. F

Hills: Middleground

1. Blend long and short stitches of 28, 3041, 841, and 3864 across the hills in the middleground. A

2. Blend in long and short stitches of 738. Then, use 1 strand of 841 to blend straight stitches from the existing 841 patches into the neighboring areas. Repeat with 1 strand of 3864 and the 3864 patch. Repeat again with 3041 and 28, creating a smooth gradient. Add 3041 straight stitches at the top of the left hill. B

D

E

F

A

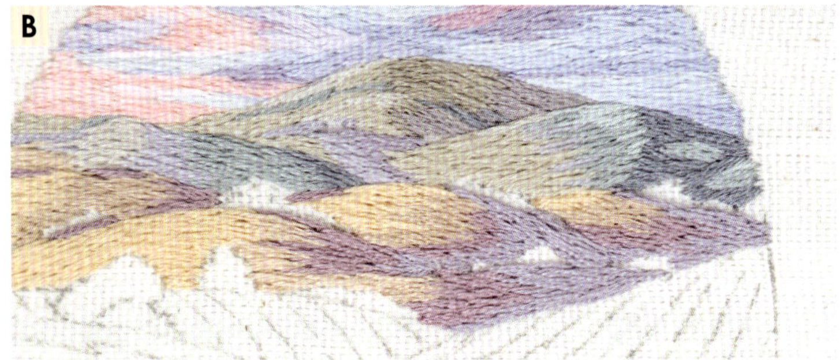
B

3. Use 1 strand of 437 to blend straight and seed stitches down the center of each hill. C

Vineyard Rows

1. Split back stitch the row guidelines on the left with 1 strand of 3051. Use 2 strands of 436 to long and short stitch between the rows, filling the open space and following the curves. D

2. Use 434 to stab and seed stitch up each row. E

3. Use 1 strand of 3041 to edge the left side of each 3051 line with split back stitches. F

4. Split back stitch the row guidelines on the right with 1 strand of 3051. G

C

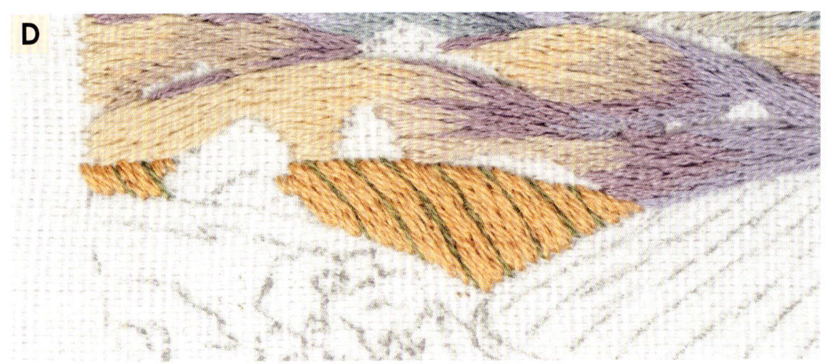
D

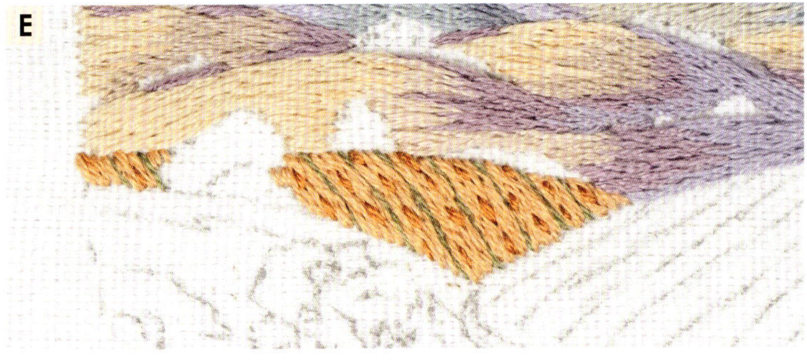
E

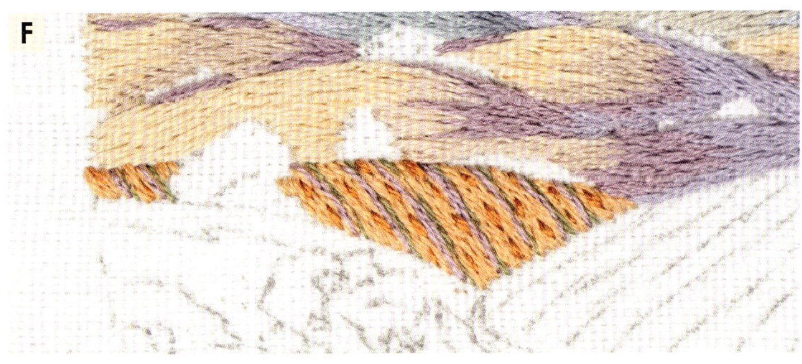
F

G

5. Fill the top half of the rows with long and short stitches of 3828. Fill the bottom half of the rows with long and short stitches of 422. Use 1 strand of 422 to blend between the top and bottom of the hill. H

6. Add stab and seed stitches in 435 on the top half of the hill. Use 739 for the bottom half of the hill. Split back stitch with 1 strand of 3041 along the right side of each 3051 line. I

Hills: Foreground

1. Blend 890, 3345, 3346, and 3347 across the foreground hill following the Color Guide. Use long and short stitches and split back stitches. A

2. Use 3364 and 422 long and short stitches, split back stitches, and seed stitches to fill in the left portion of the hill around the trees. Then, moving right across the flat ground, add long and short stitches of 988, 989, 470, 581, and 580. Leave open spaces for the flower patches on the right. B

3. Use 1 strand of 3364 and 3346 to blend seed stitches along the base of the hill. C

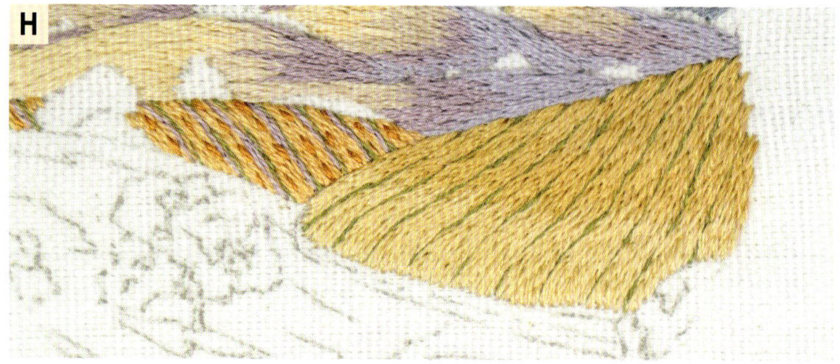
H

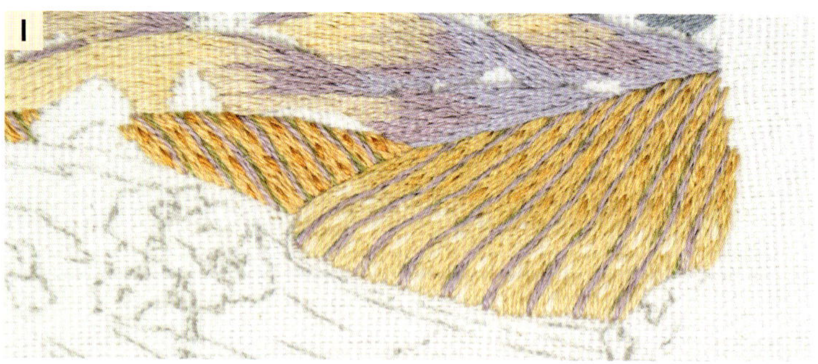
I

A

B

C

Flowers

1. Fill the 4 open spaces with horizontal 3854 long and short stitches. Use 1 strand of 3853 to shade the bottoms of the patches. Use 1 strand of 3854 to blend straight stitches into the grass and around the flower patches. **A**

2. Use 1 strand of 341 to stab stitch across the whole foreground hill, creating a dense cluster between the Step 1 patches. **B**

Road

1. Use long and short stitches of 435 to fill the area at the bottom right of the vineyard hill. Then, fill the whole road with long and short stitches of 422. **C**

2. Use 1 strand of 435 to split back stitch the existing 435 patch so it extends further to the left. Accent stitch the center of the road. Use 1 strand of 434 to seed stitch the bend in the road, then blend it with 1 strand of 435. Finally, add accent seed stitches with 1 strand of 739 in the center of the road. **D**

Trees: Background

Use 1 strand for this entire section. Make single-loop French knots anytime French knots or knots are referenced.

1. Fill in the trees on the furthest row of hills with overlapping stab stitches of 3768. Don't pull the thread all the way through the fabric, leaving a little extra height and puff on the front side of the piece. Use 501 to stab stitch the central row of trees. **E**

A

B

C

D

E

2. Stab stitch the trees on the lower right hill with 3362. Stab stitch the trees on the lower left hill and the tops of the 3362 trees with 3363. F

3. Use French knots in 520 and 3362 to fill the trees along the left vineyard rows. G

Vines

Use 1 strand for this entire section. Make single-loop French knots anytime French knots or knots are referenced.

1. Stitch over the existing row lines on the left hill with 3362 split back stitches. Then, add 3363 French knots on top of each row. A

Stitching Through Thick Work

It can be hard to push the needle through thick areas of stitching. Switch to a chenille needle with a sharper tip, and use a thimble to reduce stress on the fingertips.

2. Use 3364 to embroider another layer of French knots on each row. B

3. Repeat Step 1 on the right hill, split back stitching with 3051 and adding French knots with 3347. C

F

G

A

B

C

4. Use 471 to embroider another layer of French knots on each row. D

Trees: Foreground

Use 1 strand for this entire section. Make single-loop French knots anytime French knots or knots are referenced.

1. Fill the top left trees with French knots in 934, 520, and 3051. Accent with 3052 French knots. A

2. Move down to the central tree. Use seed stitches in 838 to stitch the trunk. Add 934 and 936 French knots to all 3 remaining trees. Then, continue filling the central and right tree with 3362 knots. Use knots of 3363 on all 3 trees. Add 08 knots to the central tree. B

3. Add 580 and 471 French knots to finish filling all 3 trees. C D

D

A

B

C

D

WOODED TRAIL

This forest scene has so much foliage and lots of repeating colors, so making use of a variety of stitch types and angles helps to differentiate the trees and bushes from one another and to create texture. Based on a photo my husband took at the Santa Barbara Botanic Garden, this project incorporates tree, bush, and rock elements (see Landscape Element Tutorials, page 30).

TOOLS & MATERIALS

- 5″ (12.7cm) embroidery hoop
- 3″ (7.6cm) display hoop (optional) and 3″ (7.6cm) circle Modern Hoopla frame (optional)
- Tapestry needle, size 26
- Chenille needle, size 26 (optional)
- Embroidery scissors
- Wooded Trail Pattern (page 159)
- Hoop stand (recommended)
- Thimble (recommended)
- 7″ × 7″ (17.8 × 17.8cm) square of natural-colored cotton duck canvas
- DMC six-stranded cotton embroidery floss (colors below)

COLOR GUIDE

TRANSFERRING THE PATTERN

Transfer the design onto the center of the 7″ × 7″ (17.8 × 17.8cm) fabric square (see Transferring Designs, page 17). Secure the fabric in the 5″ (12.7cm) working hoop.

STITCHING

Use 2 strands of thread unless otherwise noted.

DMC THREAD COLORS

					BLANC	3865	3371	3781
3790	840	3021	3864	3362	3363	3364	420	501
3052	3348	16	15	10	07	3787	471	08
838	06	3866	844	520	523	500	3051	3347
3032	3863	3860	407	758	3345	3346	580	470
704	904	734	640	645	3023	310	905	937
906	907	17	779	3064	3782	644	647	772

Sky

1. Use horizontal long and short stitches and seed stitches in BLANC to fill the open space in the center, stitching over some of the foliage. Blend in long and short stitches of 3865. Fill small spaces at the borders with satin, straight, and seed stitches. A B

Covering Guidelines

Many pattern guidelines will be covered as you stitch. Refer back to the pattern as needed.

Rock Wall

1. On the far right side, use overlapping seed stitches of 3371, 3781, and 3790. Then, fill in the wall around the existing stitches with 840, 3021, and 3864. Use 1 strand of 3864 to stab stitch throughout the section. C D

2. Use overlapping seed stitches of 3362 and 3363 to fill around the Step 1 area. Use 3364 seed stitches on the right side border. Stab stitch across the greenery with 1 strand of 420. E

Foliage: Background

1. Overlap angled seed stitches of 501, 3363, 3052, and 3348 to fill the central background foliage. F G

2. Blend in seed stitches of 16, 15, 10, and 07 to continue filling the spaces. H

Stitching Through Thick Work

It can be hard to push the needle through thick areas of stitching. Switch to a chenille needle with a sharper tip, and use a thimble to reduce stress on the fingertips.

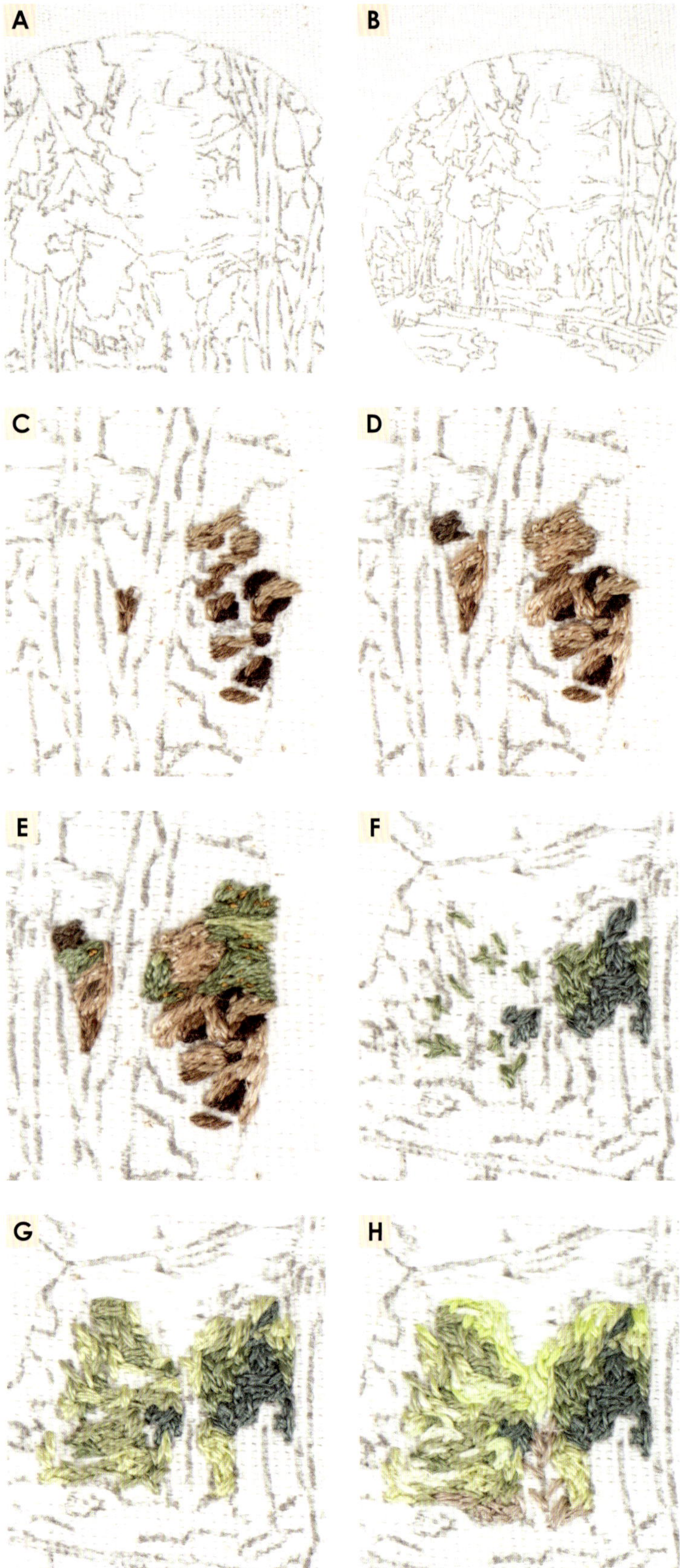

3. Use 1 strand of 3787 to split back stitch the trunks of the saplings in the same area. I

4. Seed stitch to fill the sapling on the right with 471. Accent with 1 strand of 3348. Use 1 strand of 3362 to seed stitch the sapling on the left. Use 1 strand of 3363 to stab stitch over the 501 patches. Use 1 strand of 15 to layer stab stitches across the upper left and right sides. J

Background Trees

Use 1 strand for this entire section.

1. Stitch 3 central tree trunks with 3371 satin stitches. Shade with 08 seed stitches. Stitch 3 more trunks to the left with 3371 satin stitches and long and short stitches. Shade with 838 straight stitches on the left tree, then lengthen the trunk above. Use 838 to long and short stitch and seed stitch 2 more trunks to the left. Highlight with 3790 seed stitches. A

2. Use overlapping 3362 straight stitches to continue the 3371 trunk. Add a slanted trunk with 07. Then, use 06 straight stitches and split back stitches to add a branch and highlights. Split back stitch highlights on the branch with 3866. Seed stitch shadows with 08. B

3. Use 844 to create 3 thin branches on the right side. Add tiny seed and stab stitches of 3787, 520, 3364, and 523 around the branches. C

4. Use seed stitches in 500 to shade patches in the center and between the trunks on the left. Use stab and seed stitches in 520 and 3362 to blend between the trunks on the left. Create patches above the left and central trunks. D

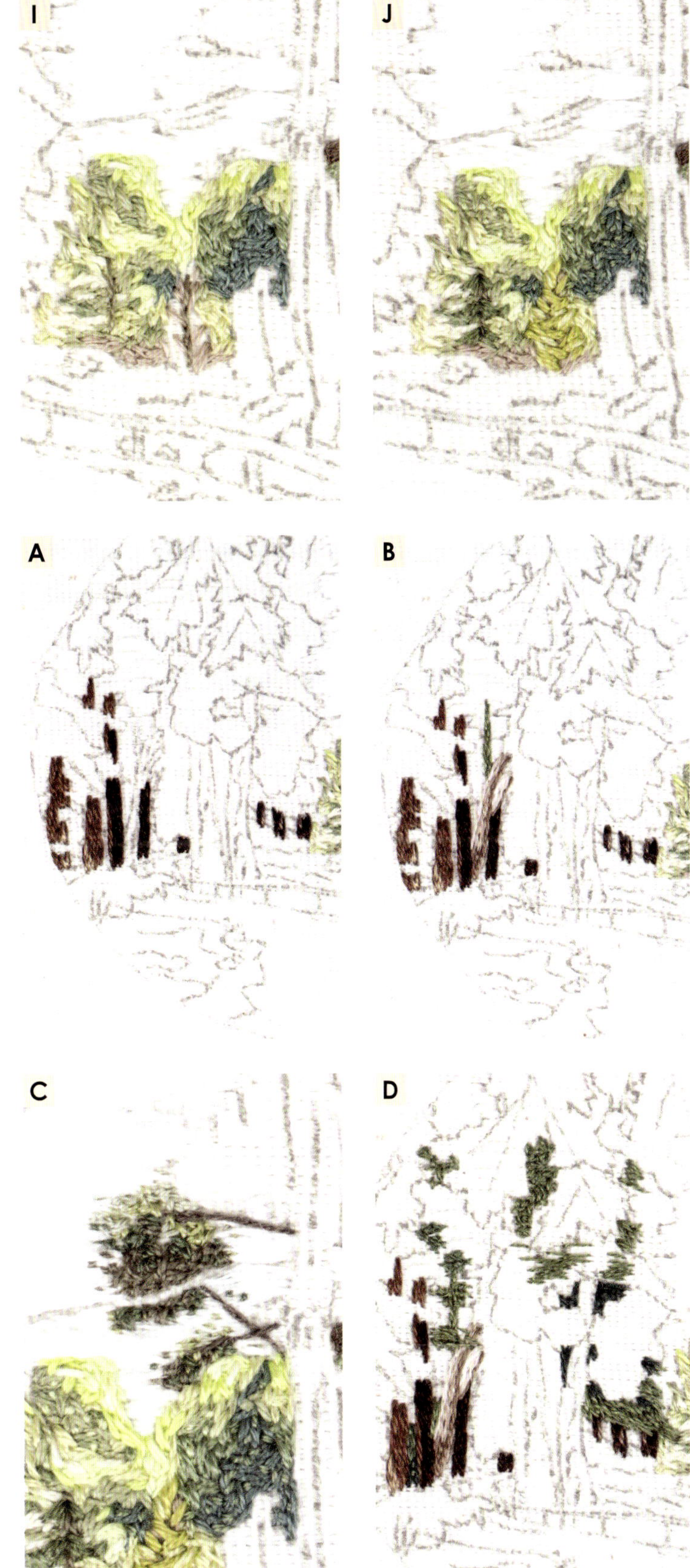

5. Add overlapping seed stitches of 3787 that blend into the center BLANC area and at the top of the design. Fill between and above the central trunks with 3363 stab and seed stitches. E

6. Blend 3363 into the central and upper 3787 patches. Then, shade the left area above and between the trunks with stab and seed stitches of the same color. Blend 523 at the top border and between the left trunks. Stab stitch 3051 into the upper left border sections. F

7. Add 3347 stab stitches to the upper left border and throughout the existing stab stitches. Fill 3052 stab stitches into the upper left border, then add seed stitches around the tree trunks on the left. Accent the central BLANC patch with straight stitches. G H

8. Blend 3348 stab and seed stitches into the area above the tree trunks and left border. Fill the tree above the short trunk with seed stitches of 520 and 3362. Accent stitch the tree with 3052 and 500. I

Foliage: Middleground

1. Fill across the ground with long and short stitches and seed stitches of 3032 and 3863. Blend in 3860 on the left. Use 1 strand of the same color to blend seed stitches in the right and center. A

2. Stab stitch across the area with 1 strand of 407, 758, and 3781. Seed stitch near the right border with 3345. B

3. Fill in more foliage at the right border and under the central trunks with 520 stab and seed stitches. Blend in 3363 seed stitches below the trunks. Then, continuing to fill the space against the right border and the center, stab and seed stitch with 3346, 3347, and 580. C D

4. Blend in 470 stab stitches at the right border. Fill on either side of the fence rail and shade the center with seed stitches. E

5. Fill the majority of the area on the right with 704 stab stitches. Blend the same color into the middle with long and short stitches and seed stitches. Finish off the space on the right with 3348 stab stitches. F

6. Blend 3052 seed stitches into the central area and remaining space on the right. Switch back to 470 to blend seed stitches on the right. G

C

D

E

F

G

7. Use 1 strand of 3863 to seed and stab stitch across the middle area. Use 1 strand of 904 to seed stitch the 470 patches around the fence and middle area. Use 1 strand of 734 to seed stitch the middle area. H

8. Use 1 strand of 704 and 3052 to begin stab stitching in the space for the sapling on the right. Use split back stitches with 1 strand of 844 to stitch the thin trunk. Shade the base with 2 strands of the same color. I

9. Continue shading the sapling with small seed stitches of 3787, 3345, and 3346. Accent with 470 seed stitches. J

10. Fill the rock at the base of the sapling with seed stitches of 844, 3787, and 640. Use 3787 and 640 for the other 2 rocks on the right border and middle. Blend 640 below the fence guidelines. K

H

I

J

K

Middleground Trees: Trunks

1. Starting with the large tree on the right, fan 844 seed stitches at the *V* and tops of the branches. Split back stitch with 1 strand to create thin branches at the top and middle. **A**

2. Blend in long and short stitches of 645 and 3790. Then, shade both sides of the tree with long and short stitches of 07. **B**

3. Blend in 3023 at the top and to fill above the V. Use 1 strand of 06 to split back stitch the left side of the large left branch. **C**

4. Use 1 strand of 3781 to seed stitch the lower half of the tree. Accent the upper part of both branches with seed and stab stitches. Use 1 strand of 645 to blend seed stitches throughout the tree. Add split back stitches along the thin horizontal branch. **D**

5. Use 1 strand of 3371 to seed stitch each large branch and the trunk. Use 1 strand of 758 to stab stitch the right branch. Use 1 strand of 06 to split back stitch along the top of the thin horizontal branch. **E**

6. Use long and short stitches and seed stitches of 3371 to fill in the middle trunk in the left area. Blend with vertical seed stitches of 310. Use 08 and 07 to shade the next trunk to the left. Then, use 07 to shade the trunk to the right. **F**

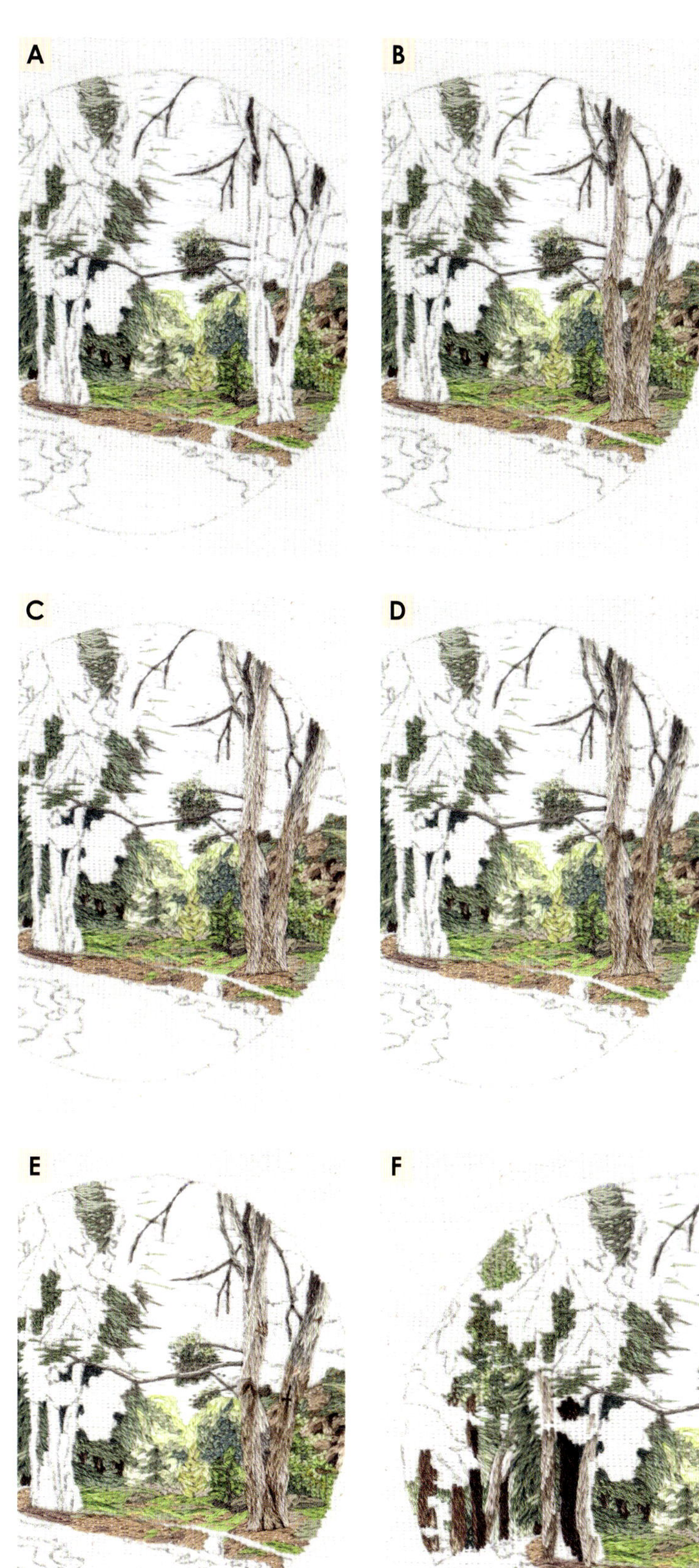

7. Use 06 long and short stitches to continue shading the left and right trunks. Use 1 strand to seed stitch the base of the right tree. Fill in the remainder of the trunks with long and short stitches and seed stitches of 3866, lengthening the stitches up toward the top of the design. Use 1 strand of 08 to seed stitch the lower halves of both trees. G

8. In the small triangle gap between these trees, create a small sapling with 1 strand of 3362, 3363, and 3364 seed stitches. H

Middleground Trees: Right

Use 1 strand for this entire section. Make single-loop French knots anytime French knots or knots are referenced.

1. Scatter French knots in 904 around the tall trunks and open space near the center. A

2. Add in French knots in 905, more fully filling the open areas of the canopy. Add in knots in 937 and 470, more densely filling on the center left.

3. Add in French knots around the center right thinner branches with more 937 and 470. D

4. Fill the lowest hanging foliage patch with French knots of 906. Continue shading upward with this color. E

5. Use 906 to add French knots to the foliage around the large tree on the right. Use 704 knots to fill in the remaining spaces of the left patches. Then, use the same color to fill around the large tree on the right. F G H

6. Fill the remaining open space at the right border and shade between the largest branches with 907 French knots. Use 16 to add knots between the largest branches of the tree, then scatter more to the left. I

7. Fill between the largest branches of the right tree with French knots in 15. Use knots in 17 to add to the foliage clusters all around the right tree, and sparsely on the foliage to the left. J

Middleground Trees: Left

1. Scatter and fill the left border area with seed stitches of 3787, 08, and 3362. Layer 779 seed stitches over the far left trunk and above. A

2. Continue layering seed stitches into the same area in 3363, 3051, 3364, and 3347. Create patches that stretch across the trunk. B

I

J

A

B

3. Fill in the remaining upper open areas with seed stitches of 3863 and 3864. Shade below with seed stitches in the same colors. **C**

4. Fill and accent the foliage with 523 seed stitches. Use 1 strand of 3064 to stab and seed stitch the foliage. Use 1 strand of 844 to split back stitch the thin branches in the remaining open area. **D**

5. Fan out seed stitches in 520 around the thin branches. Then, add in seed stitches in 3362. **E**

6. Add in 3363 seed stitches on the right and left sides. Blend in 3346 seed stitches across the branches, covering some of the French knot foliage. Pay close attention to the stitch direction. **F**

7. Add 3347 seed stitches, overlapping them and covering the fork in the branch. **G**

8. Fill in 470 seed stitches, only leaving a small open patch to the left of the thin branches. Then, fill that patch with 3364 seed stitches. Add small accent seed stitches in the same color to the bottoms of the foliage that overlap the trunks. **H**

C

D

E

F

G

H

Trail: Path

1. Use horizontal long and short stitches and straight stitches to shade in the framework for the path with 07. A

2. Fill in upper sections with seed stitches and long and short stitches of 3790. Blend straight stitches of the same color along the upper edge of the path. Blend and fill the remaining sections with 06 long and short stitches. Use 1 strand of 07 to blend straight stitches between the 06 and 07. B

3. Use 1 strand of 3064 to seed stitch the right edge of the path and into the 06 and 07 areas. Use 1 strand of 3863 to blend seed stitches into the 07 areas. Use 1 strand of 3864 to blend into the 06 and 07 areas. C

Trail: Rocks

1. Begin to shade the rocks at the right with 3787 seed stitches. Add in 645 seed stitches. Also use 645 seed stitches for the largest rock on the left of the path. D

A

B

C

D

2. Add 640 seed stitches to the rocks on both the left and right of the path. Repeat with 3032 seed stitches. **E**

3. Add 3782 seed stitches to rocks on both the left and right of the path. Use 3023 to complete the rocks on the right side. Use 644 and 647 to complete the rocks on the left side. Accent stitch below the rocks with 1 strand of 3021. **F**

Trail: Fence

Use 1 strand for this entire section.

1. Add seed stitches of 3021 to create half the fence posts. Use 640 seed stitches to shade the posts on the right and create the posts in the center. **A**

2. Add 3787 seed stitches to create the furthest posts where the path bends. Add 2 more fence posts below the trunks. Shade the existing posts with small seed stitches. **B**

E

F

A

B

3. With long and short stitches in 3032, shade the right half of the fence rail. Use split back stitches in 640 to shade the left half of the fence rail. **C**

4. Add accent stitches of 3782 along the top of the rail on the left. Blend overlapping straight stitches of 3866 into the right side of the rail. Edge the top of the rail with split back stitches in 3782. **D**

5. Accent the underside of the rail with 3371. Shade the sides of 2 posts with seed stitches. **E**

6. Seed stitch next to the second and third posts from the right with 3021. Then, blend the same color into the rail. **F**

Foliage: Foreground

1. Blend the foreground with long and short stitches and seed stitches of 08, 3790, 3863, and 3864. A

2. Continue blending to fill with 3362, 3346, and 470. B

3. Use 1 strand of 844 to create the 3 branches at the left border. Fill between them with overlapping stab stitches of 3052. C

4. Continue to fill the space with stab stitches of 3362, 3347, 704, and 16, allowing the foliage to overlap the base of the tree trunks and the path above. D

5. Fill and highlight the foliage with stab stitches in 772. With 1 strand of 3863, layer stab stitches over the ground. E

A

B

C

D

E

Patterns

All project patterns in this section and in the downloadable PDF (accessible through the QR code) are scaled to fit a 3″ (7.6cm) final display hoop. If you prefer to stitch larger, increase the size of the pattern. Every 35% increase will enlarge the pattern by 1″ (2.5cm).

Because hoop measurements vary by brand, it may be helpful to double check that the printed pattern has a diameter at least as wide as the inner hoop of the display hoop before you start stitching. This ensures your stitching will go all the way to the edges once you transfer it from your working hoop.

To access the patterns, scan the QR code or go to **tinyurl.com/11615-patterns-download**

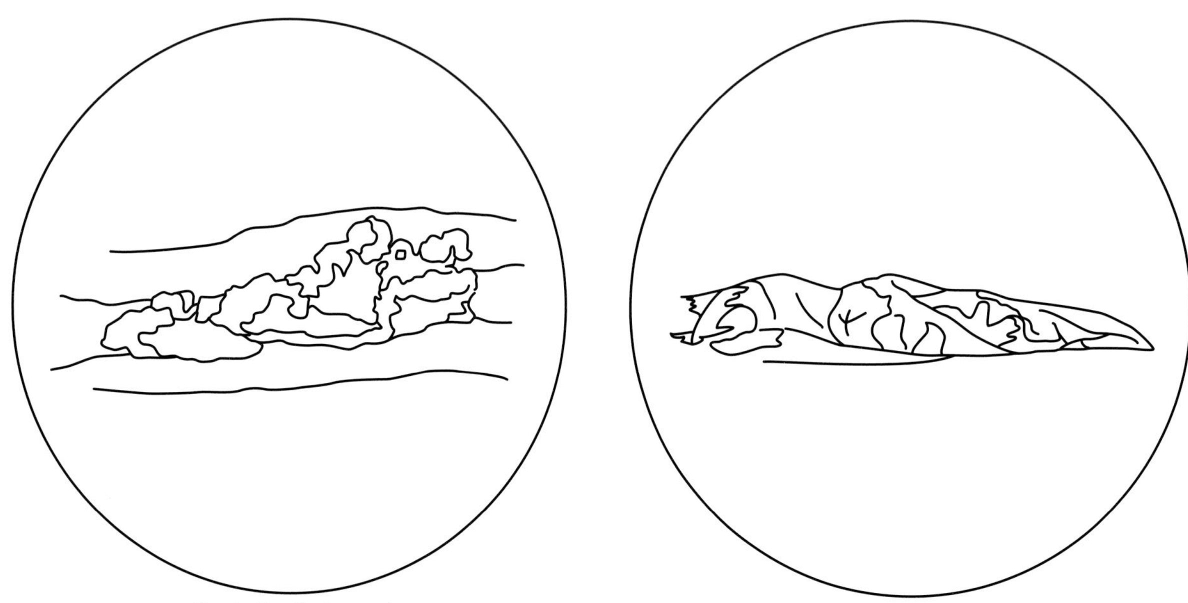

Sky & Clouds Tutorial

Hills Tutorial

Mountains Tutorial

Tree Tutorial

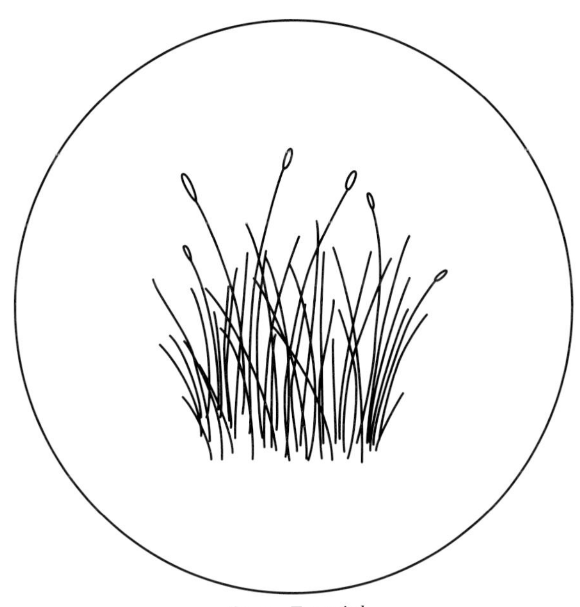

Grass Tutorial

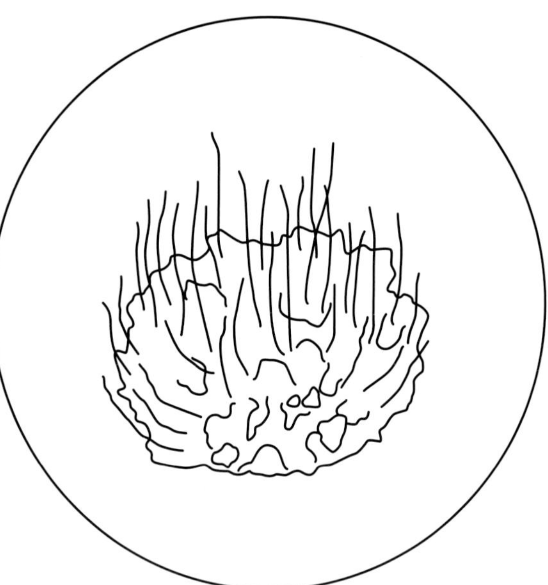

Flowers & Bush Tutorial

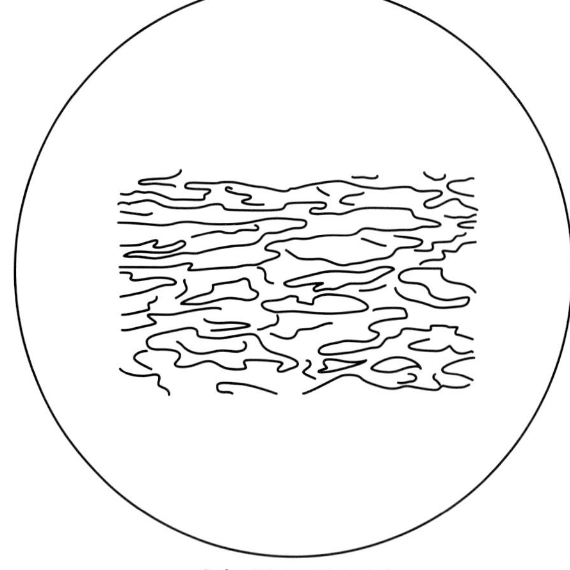

Calm Water Tutorial

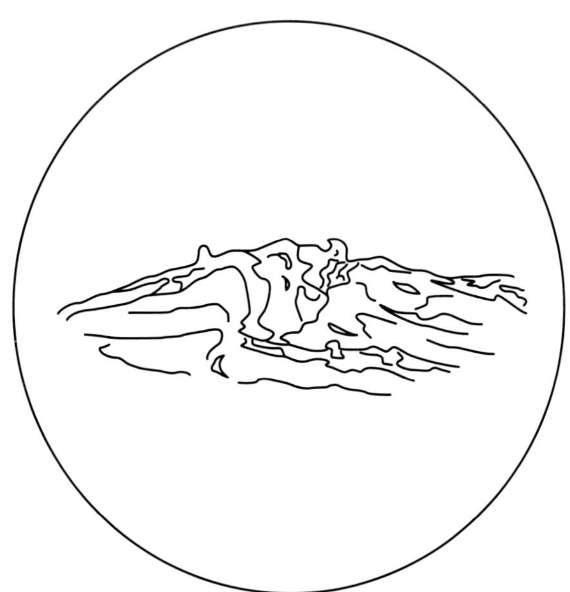

Wave Tutorial

Sand Tutorial

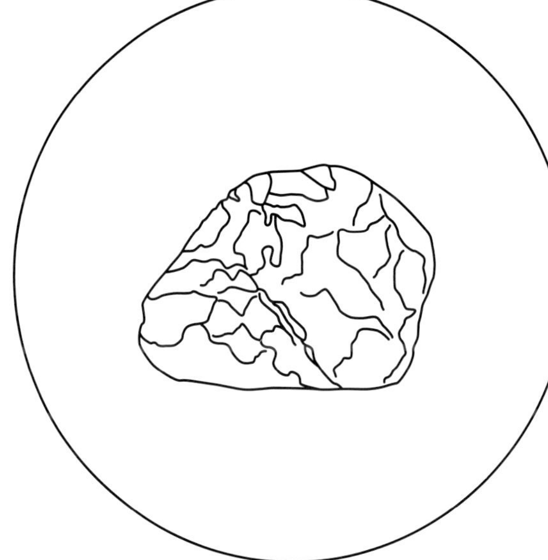

Rock Tutorial

Rolling Hillside

Seagrass Shore

Rocky Seascape

Serene Lagoon

Foothill Lake

Vineyard Valley

Wooded Trail

About the Author

Cassandra Dias was born in Santa Barbara, California in 1985, and has been creating art since she was old enough to pick up a crayon and put it to paper.

In junior high, she was introduced to mixed media collage and oil paints, and in high school experimented with new materials and mediums through ceramics and sculpture. After briefly stepping away from art in college, she decided to start creating again once she graduated, teaching herself crochet and silk screen printing. She sold her various handmade items in an Etsy shop.

In January 2020, wanting to try her hand at something new and needing a creative outlet to balance with the routine of stay-at-home motherhood, she started her self-taught embroidery journey with a bag of vintage DMC thread. She quickly became passionate about the mindful work of creating her landscapes, developing her style over the following months during the pandemic lockdown.

Her work has since been reviewed on Colossal, My Modern Met, and School of Stitched Textiles. She has been featured in print in *Love Embroidery Magazine*, *The Montecito Journal*, and *Studio Visit Book, Vol. 3* by Arts To Hearts Project. She also taught an online workshop for members of The Stitch Club on **TextileArtist.org** and presented live with Creative Spark Online Learning. Her work was recently selected to be included in a group exhibition, *Open Call: All Media 2025*, at Studio Channel Islands in Camarillo, California.

Cassandra lives and works in Camarillo, California, where she continues to produce original art pieces, and shares her love of hand embroidery on her social pages. Find her online at **cassandramdias.com** or **@cassiemdias**